Reduce Clutter, Enlarge Your Life

How to Free Yourself
from Physical and Mental Clutter
and Make Space for
More Success, Love and Fulfillment

Tom Marcoux

America's Communication Coach
TFG Thought Leader
Speaker-Author of 23 books
Blogger, BeHeardandBeTrusted.com

A QuickBreakthrough Publishing Edition

Copyright © 2014 Tom Marcoux Media, LLC
ISBN: 0615991882
ISBN-13: 978-0615991887

All rights reserved. No part of this book may be reproduced or transmitted in any form by any means electronic or mechanical, including photocopying, recording or by any information storage and retrieval system without written permission from the publisher.

QuickBreakthrough Publishing is an imprint of Tom Marcoux Media, LLC. More copies are available from the publisher, Tom Marcoux Media, LLC. Please call (415) 572-6609 or write TomSuperCoach@gmail.com

or visit www.TomSuperCoach.com

or Tom's blog: www.BeHeardandBeTrusted.com

This book was developed and written with care. Names and details were modified to respect privacy.

Disclaimer: The author and publisher acknowledge that each person's situation is unique, and that readers have full responsibility to seek consultations with health, financial, spiritual and legal professionals. The author and publisher make no representations or warranties of any kind, and the author and publisher shall not be liable for any special, consequential or exemplary damages resulting, in whole or in part, from the reader's use of, or reliance upon, this material.:

Other Books by Tom Marcoux:
- Be Heard and Be Trusted: How to Get What You Want
- Nothing Can Stop You This Year!
- Darkest Secrets of Persuasion and Seduction Masters
- Darkest Secrets of Charisma
- Darkest Secrets of Negotiation Masters
- Darkest Secrets of the Film and Television Industry Every Actor Should Know
- Darkest Secrets of Making a Pitch to the Film and Television Industry
- Darkest Secrets of Film Directing
- Truth No One Will Tell You

Praise for *Reduce Clutter, Enlarge Your Life*
• "Marcoux will help you get rid of the physical and mental clutter occupying precious space in your life. You'll reclaim wasted energy, lower your stress, and find time for new opportunities."
– Laura Stack, author of *Execution IS the Strategy*
• "*Reduce Clutter, Enlarge Your Life* gives you freedom from clutter and space for new opportunities. You increase your physical and mental stamina so you can get rid of clutter quickly. As my coach, Tom Marcoux always provides cutting-edge strategies and energizing encouragement. This book helps you reduce stress and increase success. Get this book!" – Dr. JoAnn Dahlkoetter, author of *Your Performing Edge* and coach to CEOs and Olympic Gold Medalists
• "Is clutter choking your life? This book will show you how to get rid of the clutter so that you can be much more productive. Author Tom Marcoux de-cluttered his life by getting rid of 243 big boxes of STUFF that he really no longer needed. In the process he saved a ton of money because he no longer had to rent a large storage space to keep the STUFF. He'll show you how to make the decisions. Buy this book now... because you'll use it over and over again." – Danek S. Kaus, author of *You Can Be Famous: Insider Secrets to Getting Free Publicity*

Praise for Tom Marcoux's Other Work:
• "*Create Your Best Life* is an uplifting and practical book. You'll learn skills in persuasion, charisma, confidence, influence and emotional strength—all vital elements to help you positively change the world. To make a dream come true, you'll need to get people enrolled in your vision. This is *the book* that helps you get great things done!"
– Dr. JoAnn Dahlkoetter, author of *Your Performing Edge* and coach to CEOs and Olympic Gold Medalists
• "In *Darkest Secrets of Persuasion and Seduction Masters*, learn useful countermeasures to protect you from being darkly manipulated."
– David Barron, co-author, *Power Persuasion*
• "In *Be Heard and Be Trusted*, Tom's advice on how to remain true to yourself and establish authentic rapport with clients is both insightful and reality based. He [shows how] to establish oneself as a credible expert."
-Arthur P. Ciaramicoli, Ed.D., Ph.D., author *The Curse of the Capable* and *The Power of Empathy*
• "*Nothing Can Stop You This Year* is a treasure trove of tips, tools, and terrific ideas—practical, reassuring, and energizing! Tom provides wonderful resources for achieving your goals." – Elayne Savage, Ph.D., author of *Don't Take It Personally! The Art of Dealing with Rejection*

Visit Tom's blog: www.BeHeardandBeTrusted.com

Tom Marcoux

CONTENTS

Dedication and Acknowledgments	I
Book One: Reduce Clutter	7
The Clear Clutter Process: G.E.T.F.R.E.E.	9
Reduce Clutter, Enlarge Your Life! (Overcome Mistakes)	49

Note: Guest articles by Mark Sanborn, Mike Robbins, C.J. Hayden, Dr. Elayne Savage, Rebecca Morgan, Randy Gage, Allen Klein, Craig Harrison, Dr. Martin Crous, Patricia Fripp, Linda and Charlie Bloom, and Kenneth Atchity (on various pages)

Book Two: Enlarge Your Life (Create More and Better in Your Life	57
Book Three: Nurture Yourself (Enlarge Your Life)	89
Book Four: Enjoy Life's Many Facets (Happiness, Financial Abundance, Loving Relationships and Feeling Soulfully Fulfilled)	105
A Final Word and Springboard to Your Success	199
Excerpt from *Darkest Secrets of Persuasion and Seduction Masters: How to Protect Yourself and Turn the Power to Good*	203
About the Author Tom Marcoux	210
Special Offer Just for Readers of this Book	212

DEDICATION AND ACKNOWLEDGEMENTS

This book is dedicated to the terrific book and film consultant, and author Johanna E. Mac Leod. It is also dedicated to the other team members. Thanks to Sherry Lusk and David MacDowell Blue for editing.
Thanks to the guest authors for their articles: Mark Sanborn, Mike Robbins, C.J. Hayden, Dr. Elayne Savage, Rebecca Morgan, Randy Gage, Allen Klein, Craig Harrison, Dr. Martin Crous, Patricia Fripp, Linda and Charlie Bloom, and Kenneth Atchity.

Thanks to Judita Bacinskaite for rendering the front cover. Thanks to Johanna E. Mac Leod for rendering this book's back cover. Thanks to my father, Al Marcoux, for his concern and efforts for me. Thanks to my mother, Sumiyo Marcoux, a kind, generous soul. Thank you to Higher Power. Thanks to our readers, audiences, clients, my graduate/college students and my team members of
Tom Marcoux Media, LLC. The best to you.

BOOK ONE:
REDUCE CLUTTER

Imagine being free of clutter. It's possible! I let go of 243 boxes of stuff while saving only the treasures that I truly wanted to keep. I'm here to share how I did it effectively and in minimal time.

Think of it. *How much clutter do you have to climb over before you get to what's important?* I'm talking about expanding your life and increasing your feelings of joy and fulfillment.

In the beginning of this book, I'm talking about physical clutter. In later sections, we'll talk about freedom from mental clutter. When I talk of physical clutter, I'm referring to "a crowded or disordered collection of things" (merriam-webster.com). Much of this disordered collection includes out-of-date stuff that blocks you from living at the top of your game.

With this book, I'm on a *mission to free you from clutter that beats you down and robs you of the expansive future you could have!*

How good would you feel if your living area was free of extra stuff?

This book is *different* from standard books on organizing. It is NOT an encyclopedia of organizational tips.

Instead, this book gets straight to the point and provides you with quick steps to make big progress. Such quick steps are *Clear Clutter Action Steps,* and the advantage that I'm including is: these Action Steps are designed to foster the emotional and physical stamina you need for a Clutter Removal Campaign.

Your Campaign has a bigger purpose than giving you a tidy living space. ***We're talking about Enlarging Your Life.***

Your "Enlarged Life" provides space for more love, success and fulfillment. At first glance, this may sound daunting. The second part of this book helps you shed what hinders you from really opening your life to more opportunities. The methods in this book serve to increase your personal energy.

For example, when I let go of 243 boxes of stuff, I felt physically unburdened. (I still do.) This has helped me have *more energy* for fulfilling my dreams.

Let me share with you what it's like to feel free of the burden of clutter. Because I'm not weighed down by a bunch of clutter, I have the energy to—in the same day—travel to teach public speaking at a university, work on my upcoming musical, write part of a business book, and guide my team members on my upcoming graphic novel *Jack AngelSword*. I also walk 40 minutes each day with my sweetheart to ensure our continued good health and support our relationship with daily conversation.

On the other hand, some years ago, with clutter in my way, my productivity was reduced, and I simply felt tired.

The truth is: It is great to experience the space and opportunities that you have when you take action to remove some clutter from your life. Still, I'm *not* talking about being perfect. Remove 2 or 3 boxes of clutter, and you start to feel better.

How would your life improve with less clutter? My clients and audiences mention more relaxed time with a spouse/family and the ease of knowing where everything is.

When you clear clutter, you can jump from project to project without the loss of time trying to find something. Sometimes, when addressing my college students, I share the following difference between clutter and a *resource.*
- A resource: a pen that you can find and use.
- Clutter: that pen buried and hidden underneath some pile of papers

How about you? Imagine feeling free of the clutter that crowds you out of your better life.

Let's get started. We'll use the G.E.T.F.R.E.E. process:

G - get yourself clear
E - energize yourself
T - take a big bite out
F - free up your energy
R - refuse "Time-Wasters"
E - employ help
E - embrace *Stages of Progress*

Tom Marcoux

1. GET YOURSELF CLEAR

Imagine you're facing a packed garage or heavily cluttered room. How do you feel? Many of us immediately feel drained of energy. We may experience disempowering thoughts such as "It's too much stuff" or "I hate doing this" or "I'll never get through this."

It's time to turn this around. We'll begin with:

Clear Clutter Insight:
Removing clutter requires lots of energy, and having a strategy to clearly monitor your progress supports your morale and personal energy.

It's best to use a process so that you immediately see progress and start to feel better. That takes us to . . .

Clear Clutter Action Step:
Use a Progress Log and Digital Photos to track your incremental progress.

Let's begin with my description of this strategy:

1) Pick an area to clear.
2) Take a digital photo of its original condition.
3) Devote 10 minutes (or longer) and clear the area.
4) Take a new photo of the improved condition of the area.
5) Print out the photos and place them up on a corkboard to document your progress.

If you do not have a digital camera or a camera phone or a way to print your digital photos, you could simply document your efforts with a Progress Log. Consider an entry like this:

Day   Date   Results

1   1/23   3 boxes to charity, 2 boxes to the recycling center

Simply writing down your results can serve to truly encourage you to continue!

The power of a Progress Log and especially digital photos became clear to me when I faced my own *Campaign for clearing clutter*. Some time ago, I faced a full storage locker (so big it had two doors!) filled with 221 banker boxes of material. [By the way, not all of the material was divided in banker boxes. I had to do some estimating when I assessed "the pile."]

On the first day, I removed 21 boxes; it still looked like a big pile. However, I took a digital photo that revealed the vacant space where the 21 boxes had been.

See?—Progress! I felt better and empowered to continue

my Campaign.

Another Part of "Get Yourself Clear"

Form an overall strategy. Sometimes, it's best to postpone a Campaign. Why? If you're going through some form of personal upheaval (like a break up, new job, loss of a friendship), you may want to postpone the start of your Campaign. Such an upheaval will likely drain away the energy you would have devoted to your Campaign.

Alternatively, you may need to seize current opportunities elsewhere in your life. If at this moment you were on a roll with a particular project, you might want to postpone when you start your Campaign.

For example, at one point I had a team of four people (editors and book cover designers) who helped me efficiently edit and publish two books. Having an ideal team is *not* always a given, so I just pressed forward. And I just put some material into a storage locker.

With that material tucked away in a storage locker, I now had a "clear deck." By this I mean: I was not distracted by materials blocking my path or distracting me.

Now, with a clear deck, I stepped forward and wrote seven more books in my *Darkest Secrets...How to Protect Yourself* series. [This series includes titles like: *Darkest Secrets of Charisma* and *Darkest Secret of Persuasion and Seduction Masters: How to Protect Yourself and Turn the Power to Good*]

So I strategically postponed the beginning of my Campaign. I call this "a skillful use of a storage locker." My point is that *we're talking about preventing clutter from choking your creativity and productivity*. Sometimes, using professional storage is worth the expense.

Getting Clear About "Plowing Through" or "Whittling Down"

Above I described how I plowed through sorting and removing 21 boxes of material from my storage locker. This is a preferred method for some people.

Others like to "whittle down" the pile. Perhaps, they chose to devote two hours each Saturday to sorting and discarding *some* material. This reminds me of the story of a man who wanted to expand his backyard area to build another few structures. He steadily cut a couple of bamboo trees on numerous days over a few months. In this way, he cut away a bamboo forest.

So get clear whether you want to, at this time, whittle your pile down or plow through and remove a big portion (like 21 boxes).

In summary:

Clear Clutter Insight:
Removing clutter requires lots of energy, and having a strategy to clearly monitor your progress supports your morale and personal energy.

Clear Clutter Action Step:
Use a Progress Log and Digital Photos to track your incremental progress.

Power Questions:
How will you document your incremental progress?
Will you use digital photos, a corkboard to post the images, a Progress Log or something else?

2. ENERGIZE YOURSELF

As I mentioned, your Campaign involves lots of personal energy. I've discovered a tremendous source of energy: **Your Huge Reason**. It's best to introduce this powerful resource with this account:

My client, Joseph, rented a large storage locker filled with junk—for 20 years. His wife occasionally complained about the expense.

Joseph worked long hours and explained that he did not have the energy or time to devote to reducing the amount of junk in his storage locker.

Then one day, he read a paragraph of a book that showed how one can lose thousands of dollars over a span of years while renting a storage locker. In essence, one pays so much rent that one could buy the objects 20 times over.

I asked Joseph to literally calculate how much money he would save if he reduced the size of his storage locker down to a 4 x 5 locker for only $64.00 per month.

He calculated that he could save $4,944.00 in a couple of years.

Still he was not moved.

Then, Joseph told me that one of his family members expressed her big wish was to go to Walt Disney World in 2017 and see James Cameron's Avatarland (based on the blockbuster feature film *Avatar*).

I invited Joseph to focus on the possibility of making his loved one's dream come true. "Think of how $4,944 will help you make a family trip possible," I said.

Boom! Now, Joseph had a **Huge Reason** to tackle the hassle of getting rid of a bunch of junk.

He immediately took action that day and rented the $64.00 storage locker and moved 5 boxes of "definitely keep this" material into the new storage locker. It was good that he took immediate action because he caught the last $64.00 storage locker available at that facility! He also deposited 3 bags of material at the local recycling center.

Joseph found he had even more energy because he felt irritated to temporarily pay double-rent on both the $64.00 locker and the $167.00 locker. He was frankly amazed at the energy he felt. He just had to break his personal inertia. Joseph completed his Campaign in 17 days.

Here's another example of a person using a *Huge Reason* to make a big change in the setup of her home. "Norma," someone I know, was deeply concerned about her husband "Sam," gaining lots of weight with the risk of diabetes running in his family. *With her love of her husband as her Huge Reason*, Norma got rid of 391 books and two bookcases because her husband could not walk in cold weather due to his aggravated asthma. In place of her bookcases, Norma set up a new treadmill. Now, Sam simply stepped onto the treadmill and exercised most days. His weight and general health improved rapidly with the introduction of the treadmill. Norma was empowered by her Huge Reason to make a big change in their apartment. (By the way, Norma bought herself an Amazon Kindle and started reading ebooks so she still nurtured her reading preferences.)

Special Note About Energizing Yourself: Two ways to energize yourself include:

a) *Give Yourself a Reward for any progress.* You could simply enjoy soaking in a hot bath and reading a book for 20 minutes. The difference is that you announce to yourself and, perhaps, to a family member that *you're rewarding yourself.*

b) *Note Your Progress in a Daily Journal of Victories and Blessings.* For years, I've used a Daily Journal to write down my completed tasks. I make such notes before I go to sleep, and in this way, I go to sleep happy.

In summary:

Clear Clutter Insight:
A "Huge Reason" inspires a lot of energy so you remove clutter fast.

Clear Clutter Action Step:
Explore and Find your huge reason.

Power Questions:
Who do you love most?
What do you wish for deep in your heart?

3. TAKE A BIG BITE OUT

Have you ever started a Campaign to clear clutter and after 20 minutes felt discouraged? Perhaps, you even put in two hours, but the pile still looked massive.

Years ago, someone I know, "Cindy," told me that it took her four hours to sort a banker box full of stuff. Four hours! No wonder she didn't do it. Her home was buried in clutter and her daily conversation mirrored the misery she felt. She even alienated a number of people.

But this is NOT for you!

You can do better. We'll begin here:

Clear Clutter Insight:
Keep up your morale by taking a big bite out of the pile.

This may sound like a good idea. But the real benefit comes from the following step:

Clear Clutter Action Step:
Set up your own rules so you can decide quickly and discard a big amount early on.

Cindy's problem about taking four hours to clear a banker box of stuff was tied to her rules, which bordered on perfectionism.

On the other hand, she could have different rules to shave a lot of time off the "four hours." Here are such rules:

- All computer related information over two years old gets discarded.
- All catalogues get discarded.
- All magazines get discarded.

Let's continue.

Here are examples of more rules:
- All old newspapers and magazines are sent to recycling.
- All old audio cassette programs are sent to the dump.
- All old books are sent to charity organizations. [If a book is really needed in the future, you can get an ebook copy.]

For some of us (that includes me with my habit of reading 85 books a year), letting go of old books is quite painful. So I invite you to **pay attention to your own feelings.** Be sure to have some form of emotional support. Letting go of old books can be like letting go of your "old friends." I currently use the process of *one new book in and one old book out of the house*.

Make Sure the Rules Are Really Your OWN Rules

For example, one of my friends just informed me of the predicament of her customer, "Samuel."

Samuel is now suing his daughter who dumped his three storage lockers of stuff. His daughter did *not* take into account Samuel's feelings about his materials from the past.

Samuel is furious at his daughter. Why? The loss of his stuff feels like a physical blow to him. Further, he was *not* involved. He did NOT have the chance to *Make His Own Rules* about how he would discard some of his possessions.

Start with Two Simple Rules and Discard A Big Amount Early On

Beginning with two rules can be a good springboard. For example, my client, Mary, found that two rules cleared a lot of space fast. Her rules were a) All papers that are not receipts get recycled and b) All clothes not worn in the last year go to charity. Each time she hesitated, she quickly said aloud her two rules. In just one hour she had about 10 banker boxes full of material to discard. To complete her Campaign work for the day, she went to the recycling center and then to a local Goodwill donation center. She remembered my phrase: *"Discard it and you'll never have to deal with it again!"*

[**Special Note:** Since we're talking about taking the big step of discarding material and donating material, it is a good time to make one detail clear: This book is for people who face some standard "clearing out of stuff." This book does not address the serious affliction know as *hoarding*. For more information about hoarding, you can see material offered by

http://abcnews.go.com/Health/hoarders-resources-hoarders-loved/story?id=14223831

"*Informational Sites:*

International OCD Foundation Hoarding Center
ChildrenofHoarders.com
Clutterers Anonymous
Reclaiming Dignity
Messies Anonymous
Institute for Challenging Disorganization
Online Support Groups for Hoarders:
Hoarding Forum
Stepping Out of Squalor
Help, I'm a Hoarder — CafeMom Group."]

Remember, when you set your own rules for deciding quickly and discarding a big amount early on, you'll get an emotional boost. You'll feel hopeful. You'll see the evidence that you *can* complete the Campaign!

In summary:

Clear Clutter Insight:
Keep up your morale by taking a big bite out of the pile.

Clear Clutter Action Step:
Set up your own rules so you can decide quickly and discard a big amount early on.

Power Questions:
What are big categories of items to remove?
Would the following potential rules apply in your situation?
- All magazines go to recycling.
- Most clothes not worn in the last 2 years are sent to a charity.
- Nearly all books go to charity.

4. FREE UP YOUR ENERGY

Have you noticed that clutter-removing feels exhausting? That's because it *is*. Take a moment to notice these details: When you remove clutter, you . . .
- perform physical labor
- make hundreds of quick decisions
- mourn the loss of items from your past
- feel the burden from dredging up old memories.

It's no wonder you feel drained during this process. This leads us to observe:

Clear Clutter Insight:
To clear clutter, you need lots of energy to make hundreds of quick decisions.

In the midst of my own Campaign, I discovered a necessary step so that I could efficiently keep going. After discovering that I felt exhausted after my first session of my Campaign, I *replaced my usual exercise routine* with the physical labor of lifting and moving boxes. I called it "my exercise" for a number of days when I removed clutter from my life. I *avoided* trying to tax my body with double the requirements.

Now, take a look at this step:

Clear Clutter Action Step:
Reduce your current commitments so that you reserve energy for your Campaign.

Here's example of being mindful of the number of commitments you're enduring. For many of us, the early months of the year include a new burden: preparing one's tax return. Because tax return preparation is a new, onerous chore that may also bring up tough feelings (for example, concerns about past overspending), it may be best to *postpone* your Campaign to remove clutter from your life.

Once you complete your tax return efforts, you will have an opening in your schedule. In this way, you can avoid doing two big, onerous projects at the same time.

Again, we make sure to reserve energy for your Campaign.

In summary:

Clear Clutter Insight:
To clear clutter, you need lots of energy to make hundreds of quick decisions.

Clear Clutter Action Step:
Reduce your current commitments so that you reserve energy for your Campaign.

Power Question:

What can you temporarily drop from your schedule to reserve energy for your Campaign?

5. REFUSE "TIME-WASTERS"

What are Time-Wasters? They can include:
a) people who waste your time
b) your habits that waste time

How do you quickly determine if something is wasting your time?

Ask yourself this question: ***Does this strengthen me?***

Travis' girlfriend says to him, "You know how you are. You just start a project then you run out of gas. Don't fool yourself. You're just messy."

This kind of talk not only wastes Travis' time, but it drains him of energy.

Have you noticed a friend or family member saying similar things to you? Perhaps, their comments are like these: "You'll never finish clearing out this mess." or "That's just the way you are. Clear this out, and you'll just make a bunch more clutter."

Those comments drain your energy. The solution? Avoid talking about your clutter-removing personal plans with someone who cuts you down. If that individual brings up the topic, find ways to change the topic or end the conversation.

Avoid allowing someone to lower your energy.

This relates to . . .

Clear Clutter Insight:

Guard your energy: a) avoid people who waste your time, and b) change habits that waste your time.

The first part of "guard of your energy" is to *notice* that which wastes your time and those things that weaken you. Non-supportive people weaken your resolve to complete your Campaign or even devote 15 minutes today to improving your situation.

Again, observe situations and people's behavior and ask yourself: Does this strengthen me?

Now we shift gears to asking ourselves: **Do my habits strengthen me?**

Let's talk about *habits* that waste your time. Beware of "Slow-Motion Sorting" or "Half-Awake Sorting." In a way, it can be a form of self-torture. You feel terrible while doing the sorting, and you fail to get satisfaction for making good headway on clearing out clutter. You can also make significant mistakes. So look to identify a time in your day when you're fresh and energetic for sorting.

It's better to employ a 20-minute or 30-minute session when you're fresh and able to get a lot done.

One college professor cleared out his apartment by devoting the first 15 minutes of each day to clearing clutter. This worked well for him because he is a person who feels fresh upon awakening in the morning.

Other people find that they can toss things out if they're chatting on the phone with a supportive friend at the same time. In fact, the supportive phone conversation helps them endure the pain of tossing away certain mementos—that is, those things that they ultimately want to clear out.

However, if chatting takes over your focus, it may be better to end the conversation and concentrate on **sorting quickly while listening to fast-paced music**. Then, as a reward, call your friend back after 20 minutes of *Determined and Focused Sorting*.

When you accomplish much during your 20 minutes of Determined and Focused Sorting, you feel proud of yourself. This *does* strengthen you. It even gives you an optimistic viewpoint of your life.

One of my college students recently described me as optimistic. I replied, "Thank you." And I added that I describe myself as an **Opti-Realist**. That is, I hold the view that I can improve situations in my life by devoting effective action. Such action also calls for me to be coachable. As a realist, I also know that there are certain things outside my control. I work around those details. For example, an Opti-Realist maintains the humility to face personal weakness and build a realistic and useful plan.

Part of being an Opti-Realist is to monitor how your life is going. The fast way to do this is with the question: *Does this strengthen me?*

If the answer is *yes*, then keep doing what you're doing. If the answer is "No. This actually weakens me," *stop* that behavior or event in your life.

Upon facing the realistic elements in your life, then you can form a realistic (and proactive) plan and take effective action. The optimistic part is that you hold to the faith that you can make things better. With such hope, you can accomplish a lot!

Clear Clutter Insight:
Guard your energy: a) avoid people who waste your time, and b) change habits that waste your time.

Clear Clutter Action Step:
Identify the time during the day is when you're fresh and can efficiently clear clutter.

Power Question:
Ask yourself: Does this strengthen me?

6. EMPLOY HELP

Cynthia, someone I know, has talked about developing a software application for 11 years and . . . nothing. It is not done. Why? She refuses to learn how to delegate and form some version of a team. Her regular work as a software developer saps her energy and she does not make progress on her personal project.

The truth is: often to get something big done, a person needs to grow, stretch and change.

When it comes to completing your Campaign, you may find that you simply do not have the inclination, time or energy to get the project done by yourself.

Nothing is impossible for the man who doesn't have to do it himself. - A. H. Weiler

When I mentioned "employ help" to my client Warren, he cut me off mid-sentence. Why? He proclaimed that he did not have the money to hire anyone. *The truth is: you can "hire" someone by trading value.* You can trade favors with a friend. For example, Sandra helps Mira with her taxes paperwork and in turn Mira works with Sandra to clear Sandra's clutter.

One of my mentors, the late author Richard Carlson (*Don't Sweat the Small Stuff*), told me, "Some people just don't have the eye for certain things." By this, he meant that some people *cannot* see certain details that another person *can* see! For example, I know a couple, Tim and Wendy, who simply acknowledge this fact. If Tim cleans the kitchen, Wendy knows that she will see details that Tim missed. What is clean to Tim does not line up with Wendy's preferences. So Tim does what he can, and then Wendy augments his efforts. This couple has learned to let go of trying to "educate" Tim to see what he does not see.

However, the important thing to notice is: Tim's efforts to "clean the big things" do save Wendy's time and energy. In essence, Tim is an "Effectiveness Multiplier" (my term) who helps Wendy.

Some people recall how basketball players get an "assist" from another team member. An *assist* is defined as a pass that directly leads to a basket (nba.com). Again, that's multiplying effectiveness.

Perhaps, you need one or more Effectiveness Multipliers for your Campaign.

I like to use the label "Effectiveness Multipliers" when I think about delegating and hiring help.

Now, it's time for me to introduce a valuable detail . . .

Clear Clutter Insight:
Hiring someone for two hours can give you three times the value.

If you hire a family member or a high school teen for two hours, you are likely to get *three times the value.* How?

- During the hour *before* the arrival of your helper, you'll get ready and efficiently set up things so you "get your money's worth" while the person assists you.

- During the two hours while you're working with the hired-person, you will likely move two times as fast. (I've certainly seen that happen for me. I know that I truly enjoy collaborating with another person. Also, I need to keep them busy which means I need to move fast and put things in front of them to do.)

[**Special Note:** A number of people say, "It won't help to have someone assist me. I still have to decide what category things go in." That may be true, but you can set large categories (like recycle, shred, garbage, donate to charity) and hand items off to your helper, who will place the items in the appropriate bins. Concentrate your energy on *making quick decisions*, and *avoid* getting distracted by having to search for the appropriate bins. You *avoid* having your energy siphoned off by "bin hunting." You get more done in less time.]

The above demonstrates how you can get three times the value.

Remember Cynthia's inaction that I shared above. Instead, improve your life: When you employ help, you practically guarantee that you'll make significant progress. Excellent!

In summary:

Clear Clutter Insight:
Hiring someone for two hours can give you three times the value.

Clear Clutter Action Step:

Identify who you can hire (or trade chores with) to multiply your efficiency.

Power Questions:

Who can you hire to help you get more done?

Can you trade chores and find another way to support a friend so that he or she will join in your efforts for two hours or so?

7. EMBRACE THE STAGES OF PROGRESS

What if you could gain two precious things: a) Guilt-free rest away from your Campaign and b) guaranteed progress on your Campaign?

Wouldn't that be extremely valuable to you?

My client Alicia said, "I feel bad a lot of the time."

"Why is that?" I asked.

"I'm exhausted. But when I'm not working on straightening up the house, I feel guilty."

Just at that moment, I went with my intuition and blurted out: "Oh! You don't have a *Plan!*"

"What?" she asked.

"A plan that gives you guilt-free rest and relaxation," I affirmed.

"Oh, that's not possible . . . is it?" The look on her face showed that she was hopeful that she could get out of her guilt-ridden treadmill of life.

"It is. That is, when you have a Plan. And you embrace the Stages of Progress."

At that point, we first started to identify what she found to be relaxing—so that she could have "targets" that she *wanted* to experience and enjoy. One of them was a free hour to soak in a hot bath and read a novel.

Now with "good experience-targets," Alicia was truly motivated to use the *Stages of Progress* approach.

One distinction of this process is to pre-program your periods of activity and recovery. For example, after I cleared out 243 boxes, *I set aside the next two weeks* to have nothing to do with sorting!

We're *not* robots; we do better with recovery time. One of my editors echoed this idea when she told me, "This is something our fitness teacher talks about in spin class. We alternate periods of intense work with short periods of recovery in which we focus on our breathing. We're actually *strengthening* our cardiovascular systems by doing this—as opposed to going all out the entire class period."

Now, I'll share an example of my client, Talia, who rented a house with two friends. She mentioned her plan to save money by cutting down the size of her storage locker. She wrote down this plan:

Stage 1: Donate Old Clothes and Books to Charities
(This was her way to "take a big bite out" of the pile.)

Stage 2: Bring Twenty Boxes into the Shared Garage and Sort Them
(In this stage, Talia had to leave her car parked on the street. This gave her a big incentive to move quickly and sort through the 20 boxes. First, she wanted to get her car back into the garage. Second, she wanted to avoid having her two housemates express scorn at her slow progress or procrastination.)

Stage 3: Place a Couple of Boxes in the Trunk of Her Car
(Talia designated a couple of boxes as "the hardest ones to sort." So she left them for last. Leaving these boxes in the trunk provided more weight to her car, which meant that she would lose more money to fuel expenditures. So she was motivated to sort these boxes as soon as possible.)

Stage 4: Recovery Time of Two Weeks
(As in the above example of the spin class, Talia realized that *with recovery she could come back stronger* and with a clear and ready mind.)

Stage 5: Do the Intense Sorting of the Final Boxes Left in Her Car's Trunk

The good news is that during her *Stage 4: Recovery Time of Two Weeks,* Talia actually felt guilt-free. Why? Because she had done a lot of work and achieved much. And she knew that she would pick up where she left off two weeks later.

When Talia returned to do Stage 4 Intense Sorting, she found that she had a surprising amount of energy and mental clarity; as a result, the work went much more quickly than she had projected. In fact, she said, "I was stunned at how fast I got the final work done. It wasn't so painful like I had dreaded. I'm going to remember to schedule in Recovery. And it's true! Guilt-free recovery time is awesome!"

* * *

Another Strategy: Some people set as their *Stage One: Place stuff I will definitely save into a small storage locker.* Why? In order to move around, we often need to clear the deck. So using a storage locker and setting a deadline (for closing this locker) may be a useful interim strategy. You'll be able to set things out into various categories and sort them quickly—if you have the room to do such a process.

Now, we move on to "The Next Level Stage."

The Next Level Stage is the next chapter of your life that happens after you've freed yourself from a bunch of stuff. *The Next Level Stage is about living on a new, better level.*

An essential part of The Next Level Stage is to Employ Preventative Measures to Help You Avoid Creating More Clutter

In no particular order, here are 16 *Preventative* **Measures:**

1) Use a pocket notebook in place of writing on random sheets of paper.
2) Use a *Receipts Cup.* As soon as you arrive home every day, put any receipts in one place (the cup) so that they do not intermingle with any form of clutter.
3) Place a recycle basket and shred basket next to your desktop computer and printer.
4) Buy ebooks instead of paperback books
5) Use the *One-In/One Out Plan.* Toss a book any time a new book comes into your home.
6) Employ the classic plan of setting a place for everything and returning the item back to its designated spot (immediately upon completing the use of said object).
7) Put things in a *toss in one year* box. This means that you'll discard some things if you don't use them in the intervening year. One of my editors suggested posting a

note on the object that designates when it entered the box.

8) When you put things in your pantry, highlight the expiration date so that you can quickly discard things as they expire.

9) Slow down in your purchases. Think of where the object will go and what you will discard to make room.

10) Use the philosophy of *It's just stuff.* This works for me. There have been times when I was tempted to build up a collection of my favorite feature films on Blu-ray. But then I realized it's just stuff. Having a collection is *not* going to give the exact feeling I had when I first viewed the favorite film. So if I really want to see the film again, I could call it up on Netflix.

11) Use digital storage (putting things in the Cloud) as much as you feel appropriate. Some people decide to store their favorite movies digitally, thus freeing up shelf space.

12) Avoid keeping "re-gifting items." Some of us find it very hard to "waste money" by tossing out unwanted gifts. We tell ourselves that surely these items will be valuable to someone someday, but someday rarely arrives and we're *stuck with clutter.* By the way, keep a list of items received (and person who gave it to you) so that you do *not* re-gift an item back to the original giver. It's better to donate items to charity quickly and keep your living space clear.

13) On the day some snail mail arrives, deal with it immediately. For example, I open mail quickly and sort it in the *big categories* immediately (Categories like: recycle, shred, bills, special topics like "material from the graduate school for which I'm an instructor").

14) Contact vendors that you've used before and tell them to stop sending catalogues. Do you shopping online. Let the website be your catalogue.

15) Use these *Three Principles of Less Clutter:*

a) *Buy less.* Think of this: "If I don't buy it; I won't have to clear it out!"

b) *Be sure to talk over a purchase before you make it.* For example, before I purchase a book, I discuss with my sweetheart why I'm interested in buying the particular book. In this way, I avoid buying a bunch of books when I'm vulnerable, which can happen late at night when I'm online and by myself.

c) *Avoid shopping as entertainment.* See if you can find something else to do that gives you good feelings. For example, each day, I tend to assemble part of a puzzle and listen to good music. This helps me avoid bouncing around online looking at more stuff.

16) Beware of the thought "I deserve this" because it can lead you to buying too much stuff. Instead, add a second thought like: "I'm saving my funds for experiences (taking yoga classes or vacations) instead of buying more stuff." When you have experiences, you can take photos and store them digitally, and those can inspire good memories and feelings.

Clear Clutter Insights:

a) Using *Stages of Progress* helps you make your Campaign efficient; and the Stages of Progress form your "Activity then Recovery Pattern."

b) Using strategy for preventing relapses supports your morale and new clutter-free lifestyle.

Clear Clutter Action Steps:

Write down your *Stages of Progress* and add preliminary due dates for the Stages. Be sure to include Recovery-Time between the Stages.

Write down your *Preventative Measures* to ensure your continued clutter-free lifestyle.

Power Questions:

Which Preventative Measures mentioned above appeal to you?

What other ideas can you come up with?

How will you reward yourself for incremental and continued progress?

SUMMARY OF G.E.T.F.R.E.E. PROCESS

Consider posting these details or carrying them in your pocket or purse so that they serve as a handy guide.

G - get yourself clear
E - energize yourself
T - take a big bite out
F - free up your energy
R - refuse "Time-Wasters"
E - employ help
E - embrace the Stages of Progress

- *Get clear*

Clear Clutter Insight:
Removing clutter requires lots of energy, and having a strategy to clearly monitor your progress supports your morale and personal energy.

Clear Clutter Action Step:
Use a Progress Log and Digital Photos to track your incremental progress.

Power Questions:
How will you document your incremental progress?

Will you use digital photos, a corkboard to post the images, a Progress Log, or something else?

- *Energize yourself*

Clear Clutter Insight:
A "Huge Reason" inspires a lot of energy so that you remove clutter fast.

Clear Clutter Action Step:
Explore and Find your huge reason.

Power Questions:
Who do you love most?
What do you wish for deep in your heart?

- *Take a big bite out*

Clear Clutter Insight:
Keep up your morale by taking a big bite out of the pile.

Clear Clutter Action Step:
Set up your own rules so that you can discard a big amount early on.

Power Questions:
What are big categories of items to remove?
Would the following potential rules apply in your situation?

  * All magazines go to recycling.
  * Most clothes not worn in the last 2 years to beget sent to a charity.
  * Nearly all books go to charity.

- *Free up your energy*

Clear Clutter Insight:
To clear clutter, you need lots of energy to make hundreds of quick decisions.

Clear Clutter Action Step:
Reduce your current commitments so that you reserve energy for your Campaign.

Power Question:
What can you temporarily drop from your schedule to reserve energy for your Campaign?

- *Refuse "Time-Wasters"*

Clear Clutter Insight:

Guard your energy: a) avoid people who waste your time, and b) change habits that waste your time.

Clear Clutter Action Step:

Identify the time during the day is when you're fresh and can efficiently clear clutter.

Power Question:

Ask yourself: Does this strengthen me?

- *Employ Help*

Clear Clutter Insight:

Hiring someone for two hours can give you three times the value.

Clear Clutter Action Step:

Identify who you can hire (or trade chores with) to multiply your efficiency.

Power Question:

Who can you hire to help you get more done?

Can you trade chores and find another way to support a friend so that he or she will join in your efforts for two hours or so?

- *Embrace the Stages of Progress*

Clear Clutter Insights:

a) Using Stages of Progress helps you make your Campaign efficient, and the Stages of Progress forms your "Activity then Recovery Pattern."

b) Using strategy for preventing relapses supports your morale and new clutter-free lifestyle.

Clear Clutter Action Steps:

Write down your Stages of Progress and add preliminary due dates for the Stages. Write down your *Preventative Measures* to ensure your continued clutter-free lifestyle.

Power Questions:
Which Preventative Measures mentioned appeal to you?
What other ideas can you come up with? How will you reward yourself for incremental and continued progress?

Remember to the use G.E.T.F.R.E.E. process and get clutter out of your way! Then you can enlarge your life and bring more joy to each moment and experience more success, love, and fulfillment.

* * * * * *

Above, I mentioned setting up stages. In this way, you get to feel good about *completing something.*

When I spoke with friend and colleague Craig Harrison about this book, he mentioned his thoughts about the importance of completing tasks and projects.

Here are Craig's insights:

You're Finished!
Congratulations.
by Craig Harrison

What have you finished today? What will you finish this week? This month? This year? What are you waiting for?

Look around your office. How many projects are on your desk at present? Which ones have taken up permanent occupancy? I consider my desk to be a high rent district. Squatters aren't welcome. If it stays, it pays.

After coaching from colleague John Tenza (www.coaching2greatness.com) I now awake each morning and ask myself: "What am I going to finish today?"

There's great satisfaction in completing projects, of shipping orders, of finishing manuscripts and closing deals. Conversely there's negative energy that surrounds projects with no end in sight, ones that just seem to hang on. Liberate yourself from these energy drainers. Commit to complete!

Just as the best time to make a sales call is right after you've just made a sale, so too will you feel fantastic about existing projects when you complete one of them today.

Become a Master of Time and Space

According to Tenza, a multidimensional sales trainer, "Clutter is a killer. When you put things in their rightful place, toss or give away items, you clear your mind as well as your desk and office." The key is to get into action. You must decide to do it!

Completions Not Just for Quarterbacks and Receivers

Strive for completions. Coach Tenza knows: "Completions give you freedom from that gnawing stress that something needs to be done. Each time you complete an existing project you create new space and new energy for yourself." John and I concur: your brain and body will thank you or the successes you will realize through completions.

On Becoming A Terminator

Here are some tips to complete more projects.

- Calendar time for projects and their completion.

- Go public with dates for completion of milestones.

- Defer gratification; link your own rewards to completion dates.

- Stagger projects to make regular progress on short, medium and long-term projects weekly.

- When you get stuck, get help; ask for second opinions, reviews or assistance to avoid losing momentum.

- Track your progress with flow or pert charts, calendars or other schemes that allow you to visualize your success.

- For difficult tasks within projects, break them down further into more manageable parts.

- When feeling stuck, change your body chemistry. Exercise and you will energize yourself and have renewed vigor for completing projects.

There are many ways to reach the "end" zone—incremental progress or leaps and bounds. Look anew at your desk, your to-do list and your yearly goals and build your completions.

Congratulations…you've finished this article. What else will you finish today?

Craig Harrison's Expressions of Excellence!™ helps organizations express their sales and service excellence and its professionals become better communicators and leaders. His presentations, books, courses and coaching empower adults worldwide to shape their world. Based in the San Francisco Bay Area Craig travels the world as chief expressionist to foster excellence for you! For more information visit www.ExpressionsOfExcellence.com or call (510) 547-0664.

REDUCE CLUTTER, ENLARGE YOUR LIFE! – YOUR GUIDE TO SUCCESS AND HAPPINESS (OVERCOME MISTAKES)

This book began as an article that I wrote for my blog at www.BeHeardandBeTrusted.com. Now, here is that article:

The greatest need of our time is to clean out the enormous mass of mental and emotional rubbish that clutters our minds.
– Thomas Merton

How is your life going?
Are you experiencing the freedom that you hoped for?
Many of us are choked by clutter, which is blocking us from the vital actions that can enlarge our life.
Years ago, when I met her, author Barbara Sher told me: "Adults can do what they want because they clean up the messes."
Now, I ask you:
Are you spending all of your time and energy in cleaning

up messes?

The truth is: you need to be skillful about clutter—both physical and mental clutter.

It comes down to realizing:

How much clutter do you have to climb over to get to the vital actions that enlarge your life?

And –

How much mental clutter do you have that prevents you from experiencing happiness?

This concept is so important to me that I "paused" a number of projects so that I could write this section.

Here I will share *3 Big Mistakes and 3 Effective Actions.*
Let's begin:

1. Realize "Go it alone and you go slow."

The idea that you must handle your clutter only by yourself can be a big mistake! Why? Because we're all down on the planet for a reason. To help each other. If you have a problem with your car, you see a mechanic—yes?

If I need a book cover designed, I see a graphic artist.

Like you, I could put time into studying something that is not connected to my natural talent, but that would be wasteful. Make sure that you strengthen your strengths.

And when it comes to clutter, you don't have to deal with it only by yourself.

It can be as simple as telephoning a friend. You both can agree to have a light conversation while you sort some receipts or other paperwork. Your friend could even be talking to you while she is walking on a treadmill at her own home.

Or you could set up a trade of efforts. Your friend could help you sort your packed closet for an hour and then you could make him a nice dinner (or treat him to a movie).

Or you could hire a friend (at an "okay" or "friend-rate" of pay)—or hire a professional to help you.

Now, you may say, "I don't have extra money to put toward getting someone to help me with clutter."

Yes, I've heard that from people who are still stuck 5 to 10 years later.

Here's a secret. When I hire someone to help me sort, the work goes 3 times faster. Why? Because money is flowing out while the clock ticks. You bet I'm going to get my money's worth. By the way, I've heard from a number of people: "My sorting is so complicated. No one else can do it for me."

My response is: "Okay, you do the sorting and hand items to your helper for recycle, shred and file."

Again, when I have someone standing there—I personally move faster. Years ago, I heard someone say, "Clutter is the result of unmade decisions." I am decisive when I have someone helping me.

There is an old phrase: "Jumping over dollars to pick up dimes." You need to concentrate most of your time on high-yield activities related to your strengths.

You see:

you spend time on clutter,

but you *invest* time in your area of strength and talent.

A writer needs to write. A dancer needs to dance. A painter needs to paint.

Mistake #1: Trying to handle clutter only by yourself.

Action #1: Ask for help; hire help; get a jump start.

2. Ramp up small targets and log (and photograph) your progress.

What's a small target? How about clearing the space

immediately in front of your computer monitor?

Here's the big mistake: Setting too big a target, losing heart, and giving up.

In one year, I wrote and had published 3 books (a total of 1,258 pages). How? A simple principle that I coined:

Keep score and achieve more.

After every session of writing, I use the "word count" function in MS Word. I log how many words I wrote. I print out pages and place them in a binder. I literally see my progress—and it fills me with enthusiasm, hope and energy.

Here's the secret: When it comes to clearing clutter, a little progress often looks like "no progress." A room that is packed with clutter still looks full of clutter—even though you took two garbage bags of clutter out of that room.

That's the reason that you need to use the *keep score and achieve more* strategy.

Take photos with a digital camera or your smart phone. Take a photo of each little area that you clear. Print the photo and place it on a corkboard (perhaps, tack the corkboard up on the back of a door). Otherwise, you could keep such photos in a folder on your computer or create a collage and use it as a "wall" on your desktop.

Start with small targets for clearing clutter:

a) clear the space immediately in front of your computer.

b) clear the floor next to your nightstand.

c) set up a filing system

Remember, take a photo of each accomplishment.

Where does hope come from? From you!—when you can see your progress.

Mistake #2: Setting too big a target, losing heart, and giving up.

Action #2: Set a small target and log (and photograph) your progress.

3. Enjoy happiness

Let's face this together. Many times, we have mental clutter that prevents us from experiencing happiness. How? It's connected to the "rules" that we set on an individual basis.

Do you know someone who says (or thinks): "I can't be happy until I clean up the kitchen."

That's a "rule." And it can cause pain and feeling dead inside.

Why?

Because if you're a parent, work a job just for the rent, and do your hobby (that you'd like to be your eventual job), then you're really busy!

Ask yourself:

How much mental clutter do I have to climb over before I can feel happy?

By the way, I felt happy just typing that above question. Do you know the reason? It's because I derive joy at being at your service—and connecting with you through this section.

Do you get to experience happy moments and fulfillment each day?

You can feel that way when you use strategy instead of defaulting to mental clutter and disempowering "rules."

I have another question for you: Can you be happy *while* you're cleaning up the kitchen?

Here's a better question: *How* can you be happy while you're cleaning up the kitchen?

Some helpful ideas:

a) Call a friend and talk while your clean up.
b) Listen to energizing music.

Where is happiness?

It is in this present moment.

That's the only place we experience happiness—because when you "time travel" to the future (worrying about the future) or to the past (feeling guilty over mistakes of the past)—you are not here!

The solution is: *Observe the Mental Clutter—and let it float on by.*

A "rule" can simply arise in your thoughts. Cindy thinks: "My sister should appreciate how I found that book for her and say, 'Thank you.'"

In the work of W. Timothy Gallwey, we see three questions:

- What don't I control here?
- What am I currently trying to control?
- What could I control that I'm not presently controlling?

Does Cindy control the behavior of her sister? No.

What is she trying to control? Her sister's behavior and her sister's values.

What can she actually control? Her own thought processes.

Cindy can let her thoughts about what her sister "should do" just float on by.

Trying to control others is mental clutter. Let it float on by.

Then you can enjoy more moments of life.

To enjoy more moments together, a couple, Leeta and Jorge, often say, "Save that for the couple therapy session." In this way, they can avoid much bickering and enjoy most of their week—because they choose to have the tough discussion during their couple's therapy session.

Focus on this: "What am I happy about right now—this minute?"

Another helpful question is: "What am I grateful for?"

Mistake #3: Setting a rule that puts clutter between you and feeling happy.

Action #3: Ask: "What am I happy about right now – this minute?"

* * *

Focus on these details:

Mistake #1: Trying to handle clutter only by yourself.
Action #1: Ask for help; hire help; get a jump start.

Mistake #2: Setting too big a target, losing heart, and giving up.
Action #2: Set a small target and log (and photograph) your progress

Mistake #3: Setting a rule that puts clutter between you and feeling happy.
Action #3: Ask: "What am I happy about right now–this minute?"

Take positive action and *you'll feel better.*

Tom Marcoux

BOOK TWO:
ENLARGE YOUR LIFE (CREATE MORE AND BETTER IN YOUR LIFE)

One can never consent to creep when one feels an impulse to soar. - Helen Keller

Now that we've covered material that helps you tame the "clutter tiger," let's make sure that you have the methods for truly enlarging your life.

Earlier, I asked this question:

How much clutter do you have to climb over to get to the vital actions that enlarge your life?

Now, let's answer this question:

Are you taking daily action to enlarge your life regardless of any clutter that may remain?

Say *yes!*

Now, we'll explore six topics to improve your skills and keep your business interactions positive:

1) How to Transform Your Life to Total Success!
2) One Yes for Infinite Success

3) How You Can Write Your Own Destiny
4) Clarity and Nurturing to Power Up Your Success
5) Go for Your "Home Run" for Real Success
6) Secrets of the Hidden Side of Great Success

Topic #1
Book Two: Enlarge Your Life (Create More and Better in Your Life)
How to Transform Your Life to Total Success!

Do you, deep in your heart, want a much higher level of success?

Feel something is missing from your life?

Here's a useful principle: *Consistency Creates Success.*

How do you "do" consistency? I'll give you one of the best methods I know: *Use a Success Log.* In a Success Log you write down details of your progress accomplished each day.

Here is an example. At present I'm writing a book. Here's a recent entry in my Success Log:

My current book that I'm writing:

Day	Date	Result
30	2/1	up to 35,689 words

This is part of my process, and I have 23 books on Amazon.com.

Here's another example.

One of my clients is working on her taxes paperwork.

Day	Date	Result
12	1/27	15 minutes sorting receipts

The title of this article is "How to Transform Your Life to Total Success!" **And the answer is:** *Set up a few Success Logs;* that is, pick the vital areas of your life and identify something to measure.

You can also use a Success Log for important details for the health and happiness of loved ones. For example, I keep a log of how many days I successfully encourage and inspire my sweetheart to walk. I'm concerned that she remain healthy and avoid diabetes which runs in her family. So I encourage her to take a daily walk with me. I log how many times per week that we do accomplish that daily walk.

I use a corkboard near my desktop computer and post Success Logs. Some of my Success Logs include:

1) Daily Exercise
2) Progress on *Jack AngelSword* (graphic novel)
3) Progress on business book
4) Progress on self-help book
5) Progress on business paperwork

Good ideas are nice. However, **consistent action is what makes the true difference in achieving success with those good ideas.** (For more about getting into action and overcoming procrastination, see a free chapter of my book *Nothing Can Stop You This Year!*—at Amazon.com)

Recently, best-selling author Randy Gage provided a guest article for this book [yes—I'm tracking my word count]. So I looked up some of his best advice:

Randy Gage says, *"I get a financial statement—my financial net worth—every month . . . I want to know every month that I've made some progress toward being wealthier . . . I need to see that every month and that keeps me focused, keeps me in the game everyday, because I see I'm always making progress. So give yourself benchmarks to track; give yourself some kind of accounting system like that. And then be consistent."*

Some would say, "That's the reason that Randy is a millionaire and others are not: He measures his progress every month in financial matters."

Now it's your turn. What are important areas of your life? Some examples:
- Health—Log daily exercise
- Spirituality—Log daily prayer/meditation sessions
- Love Relationship—Log how many compliments you give your partner per week
- Career Goals—Log networking activity on LinkedIn and attending networking events
- Financial Goals—Log all expenditures and forms of income
- Fun—Plan and do something fun each day (even something as simple as 15 minutes of assembling a puzzle and listening to music).

You can achieve your personal "Total Success" by having Success Logs for the vital few elements of your life. Track your actions.

Remember: *Consistency Creates Success.*

Get started today!

* * * * * *

Topic #2
Book Two: Enlarge Your Life (Create More and Better in Your Life)
Use "One YES for Infinite Success"

Have you ever thought of someone who could say yes and change your whole life? Imagine knowing how to get the "One YES" that improves your life. We'll use the O.N.E. process:

O – open your thoughts
N – notice a category
E – energize your contacts

1. Open your thoughts

What would be your "One YES" that massively improves your life?

For some it would be "Yes, we'll publish your book."

Others would welcome:
- Yes, I'll marry you.
- Yes, I'll invest in your company.
- Yes, I'll join your team.

Have you noticed that some people refuse to even speculate about the possibility of something great happening? Why? Perhaps, they're trying to avoid feeling disappointed.

The truth is life brings disappointment even if we try to hide and hold tiny expectations.

For many of us, it is better to have a "glorious direction" to aim for.

When I say, Open Your Thoughts, I invite you to ask this question: "What would make that person who can give the 'One YES' take special notice of me and my project?"

It could be:

a) You sold 20,000 copies of your graphic novel.

b) A notable person endorses your book.

c) A doctor has certified that your meditation audio program helps her patients.

Big possibilities begin when we open our thoughts to new ideas. Have the courage to imagine who can change your life with a "Yes" response. Then start preparing so you can impress that person and get their cooperation.

2. Notice a category

Thinking of only ONE person and trying to be perfect in one meeting to get their cooperation may feel overwhelming. If I concentrate on only ONE person who can change my life, then I might be terrified of making a mistake.

There is a solution: Instead of thinking of only ONE person, I shift my thoughts to thinking of how I can contact a whole "category of people" who could say yes.

So now, I'm *not* worrying about just one person and one meeting. I now realize that I can reach out to a whole *number of people* who are in the same category. It's a whole bunch of people who share a trait or two.

For example, when I enter a negotiation, I think, "Let's see if they want to play." In this manner, I reduce my level of nervousness. Sure, in any important meeting, we're likely to retain some nervousness. The target is to *reduce the amount* of nervousness. You're, in essence, telling yourself, "I will have more chances and opportunities. Not only this one meeting."

3. Energize your contacts.

First, let the right people know what your big goals are. You've probably heard of the theory of "Six Degrees of Separation," which holds that everyone is merely six steps away. So all you need is an introduction from one person to another.

I know that this can work in your favor because it's worked for me. For instance, when I first began in the film industry, I wrote a screenplay that one software engineer handed to another software engineer—then to a real estate developer—and then to the California Motion Picture Commissioner.

When I needed it, the California Motion Picture Commissioner arranged for San Luis Obispo airport and an American Eagle airplane (for free) for a feature film I was directing.

Currently, my team is focused on our three franchises (all

include graphic novels and feature films):
- *Crystal Pegasus* (children's fantasy)
- *Jack AngelSword* (fantasy-thriller)
- *TimePulse* (science fiction)

My ultimate goal is for all three franchises to serve millions of people so near the end of my life, I can sell my company to . . . you guessed it: Disney.

Why? Because I want my three franchises to continue to inspire and serve people beyond my lifespan.

Second, while you are developing your network of contacts, focus on what I call the *3 Magic Words of Networking: Help Them First.* Find a way to be supportive of what the other person is doing. Develop warm connections.

You help others by:
- listening to them (that's supportive)
- asking "How can I be supportive of what you're doing?"
- asking "Who is your ideal client?"
- helping people connect with what they need (for example, someone needs a graphic artist and you connect the person with a skillful and trustworthy graphic artist you know)

Here's an example. Some weeks ago, a professional speaker asked me about how to have his books printed and distributed. I provided a valuable response to his question. Then, later, out of the blue, he connected me with a venture capitalist.

When you learn about what support a person needs, see if you can provide some help. Even just listening, is helpful. We all feel better when someone shows care by listening well to us.

So in essence, I'm saying:

Energize your contacts.

You can make big things happen with the right people on board, and you can get the right people on board by helping them first.

* * * * * *

Topic #3
Book Two: Enlarge Your Life (Create More and Better in Your Life)
How You Can Write Your Own Destiny

Wouldn't you like to write your own destiny and live the life of your dreams? We'll use the P.E.N. process:

P – play for the long term
E – encourage others to see your skills
N – nurture coaching; drop "dark-criticism"

1. Play for the long term

Just recently, a contact at LinkedIn.com was informing other authors (in a LinkedIn.com group) that the chance of a having one's book turned into a feature film was nearly zero.

I decided to add the following comment to the conversation at LinkedIn:

"I speak from the experience of
- writing, directing, producing a feature film that went to the Cannes Film Market and that gained international distribution (including Taiwan, Hong Kong, Poland, Buenos Aires, etc.)
- having written 22 books
- guest lecturing at Stanford University
- lecturing as a graduate school/college instructor (six classes)
- appearing as a guest expert on TV, radio—in magazines

(like Streaming) and newspapers [labeled as "The Personal Branding Instructor" by The San Francisco Examiner]

One thing I know for a fact: if one does not put work out into the world, one has no chance to move forward.

If you're concerned about writing well enough, hire an editor. For example, I hire 3 editors for each non-fiction book I write. Why? Often, they're editing different sections simultaneously [I separate books into sections I call "Book 1, Book 2, etc."].

Now, I'm focusing on 3 franchises that I have created for my own company.

- *Crystal Pegasus* (children's fantasy—1st graphic novel of the trilogy on Amazon)
- *Jack AngelSword* (fantasy thriller—graphic novel, illustrations being refined now)
- *TimePulse* (science fiction)

When I sat down with my attorney (chairperson of the entertainment division of a top Los Angeles firm), we talked about my above three franchises. I mention this because, as we all notice, Hollywood loves trilogies.

I shared the above as an example of "playing for the long term."

* * *

My point is that many people will give up too soon.

Instead, I invite you to play for the long term. Have a long term goal and keep going through the years of ups and downs."

Many of life's failures are people who did not realize how close they were to success when they gave up. – Thomas Edison

A number of people were shocked when film director Joss Whedon was handed the reigns of the big budget feature film *Marvel's The Avengers*.

Joss commented, "I wanted to say 'quit [doubting me].' At that point, I had been a professional [TV/film] writer for 24 years."

Joss has played for the long term, and it certainly has paid off for him, Marvel and movie fans.

2. Encourage others to see your skills

Several years ago, Joss Whedon knew that it was unlikely that a film studio would have given him a feature film to direct. So at the beginning of his career, he produced a TV show *Buffy, the Vampire Slayer* and he directed a couple of episodes per season. In this way, he put himself through a form of practical film-directing "school."

All along the way, people with power in the film industry could see how skillful Joss was becoming.

Now it's your turn. How can you show people your skills in some small way? If you want to direct feature films, how about directing a short film and placing it up on YouTube.com?

Another example: Edgar Allen Poe, Deepak Chopra, and Sigmund Freud all self-published their first book.

Will you self-publish some work?

3. Nurture coaching; drop "dark-criticism"

Some people will offer you what they call "constructive criticism."

It's important for you to identify if the person is offering useful coaching or if they're merely slamming dark-criticism your way.

Dark-criticism is meant to hurt you, not build you up.

What shocks me sometimes is that friends and family can slam us with dark-criticism.

Why do they do this? In some cases, these critics have subconscious jealousy that comes out as what they call advice ("I'm just trying to help you/protect you").

Watch out for this garbage!

Here's something useful. Go to people for advice who have already accomplished what you want to accomplish.

These accomplished people can offer real and useful coaching.

If you're having trouble distinguishing if advice is coaching or dark-criticism, ask yourself these questions:

a) Does this person want the best for me?

b) Is the person absorbed in their "own story"?

c) What does this person gain if I give up and step away from my own dreams?

* * *

You can write your own destiny. Many of us find that we're co-creators of our lives with Higher Power and the universe.

Remember to use the P.E.N.:

P – play for the long term

E – encourage others to see your skills

N – nurture coaching; drop "dark-criticism"

Express your creativity and enjoy your life.

* * * * * *

Topic #4
Book Two: Enlarge Your Life (Create More and Better in Your Life)
Clarity and Nurturing to Power Up Your Success

Ever feel that a friend or family member is subtly cutting you down or holding you back?

Here's what can help. Consider these questions about the situation:

1) Is this really support, or is it something else?

2) Is it fear that you're disruptive to *their* life?

3) Do they label you as "annoying" because you threaten *their* self-esteem?

The truth is: for you to have a joyful and fulfilling life, you will do extraordinary things. You'll need to stay strong. Having support can be so vital. With my clients, I emphasize: "Put effort into having a real support system."

[Before I go further, I want to add that sometimes, we do need help to expand our perspective. I have hired coaches and I have had mentors who have helped me see more sides to the process of being creative and building a business. So sometimes, a person who truly cares about us will give us coaching that includes important but tough news to hear. However, my topic here is about an insidious phenomenon: the family member or friend who subtly drains our energy.]

Beware of a friend or family member who somehow sabotages your small steps forward.

For example, a friend of a friend of mine, "Cheryl," had a husband who cut down her aspirations to start her own business. Eventually, Cheryl gave up and sold her equipment that she had in the garage. Then, her husband left her for another woman. I say, "Good riddance!" Cheryl is still grieving, but I'm hopeful that she'll renew her interest and efforts for creativity and entrepreneurship.

Here's another example. One of my clients, "Sharon," had a friend who called her "cheap." What was Sharon's crime? Treating her cynical friend to burritos.

I celebrated when Sharon stood up to that friend and said, "Look, I need to conserve my cash so that I can hire people to help me make my dream business come true. You can easily eat expensive dinners with your other friends."

By the way, Sharon's so-called "friend" ended their friendship. Again, I say, "Good riddance!"

My point is: clarity is important. You need to be able to see if you're being helped or hurt by people you care about.

Sometimes, we simply have to face facts that someone we care about does not care or maybe does not have the capacity to truly support us in our new adventure to expand our horizons.

So be it.

My friend, become your own best friend and nurture yourself. (For more about nurturing yourself, please see my book, *Love Yourself to Financial Abundance and Spiritual Joy*.)

If a family member consistently puts you down, see if you can minimize your time and interactions with that person.

Better keep yourself clean and bright; you are the window through which you must see the world. – George Bernard Shaw

Remember, when you nurture yourself, you can make a kind contribution to the world. And that is helpful to us all.

* * * * * *

Topic #5
Book Two: Enlarge Your Life (Create More and Better in Your Life)
Go for Your "Home Run" for Real Success

Ever find yourself so busy doing what's necessary to pay bills that you think: "How am I going to leap out of this rut?" I've learned that it takes unusual and sometimes extreme effort to work on something that will make a Big Difference in your life. This special something, I call your "Home Run." Sometimes, I call this Home Run by another name: a Big Leap-Goal. We'll talk about how you can take action for your Home Run.

To stay on top of bills, you takes "small steps": get a job to pay the rent or get some immediate clients. But do you ever take the time to think of a Home Run?—Something that can have a Big Payout?

A Home Run (or "Big Leap-Goal") could be something that really employs your talent and innate abilities—and which could result in significant prosperity.

Here are four examples:
1) One of my friends is an excellent writer. Currently, he is doing a crowdfunding campaign for the production of a play based on a manuscript he wrote. He aims to make a living as a writer (a Home Run) and to write a series of books in the same genre as his play.
2) Another friend seeks to be a feature film director (a Home Run). She is currently preparing a small film that she will post on YouTube.com. To this, I say, "Bravo!" She is showing, in a small way, what she can do. She is, in essence, saying, "Hello World, here is what I can do. And I'm looking for my next opportunities."

3) One of my clients is launching a series of Podcasts. Why? She aims to have 300,000 downloads a month. Then from this audience, she'll draw people to attend her two-day seminars. At $2,000 per person and with 50 people attending a seminar, that's $100,000 (a Home Run).
4) Another client wrote 52 blog articles and incorporated them into a book (a Home Run). She has just launched her speaking/writing career.
5) In an earlier blog post, I wrote about taking action for your "One YES for Infinite Success." [Someone says, "Yes"—and your life massively improves.] Now, I'm going to go deeper into what actions are necessary.

You need to take action for *4 Vital Steps.*

If you fail to manifest these 4 Vital Steps, it's likely that you'll miss an opportunity to get that One YES for Infinite Success. Here is the L.I.S.T. of what is necessary to gain the One YES.

L – listening
I – involved credibility
S – significant rehearsal
T – trustworthiness

1. Listening

So many opportunities are lost because people are failing to make warm connections. How? They're not truly listening to each other.

Why? Listening is hard work.

Researchers note that true listening is contrary to much of human conditioning. Data suggests that portions of the human brain are focused on survival (the "reptile brain") and preventing loss (the "emotional brain").

So what happens? Someone says something and our brain automatically judges the message as to whether it threatens our survival or might cause some loss (perhaps, discomfort or a loss of self-esteem).

So in essence, it's automatic to view something with negative judgment.

How can we rise above this and develop true listening?

For one thing, just observe your first thought or judgment when someone is talking. Take a deep breath and keep listening.

2. Involved credibility

To do something that will make a big positive difference in your life, you need credibility. You need people to say Yes to you. Often, they want to know who has hired you in the past. Who has believed in you and seen that belief yield positive results? You need to be involved with people — serving them, helping them make good things happen.

Much of your credibility may be built on "third party endorsements." For example, when I raised funds for my first feature film, I built on the fact that I had won a special award at the Emmys.

How can you take action and get involved with projects? Or will you begin a project and gather people to help you?

3. Significant rehearsal

To get the One YES, you need to demonstrate your confidence — and that takes rehearsal. With my college level public speaking students, I invite them to imagine a grandmother saying, "Feeling fear? Rehearse, my dear."

To speak with confidence, there is no substitute for rehearsal.

Do you have a tough conversation coming up with a loved one? Rehearse saying things in a calm, supportive manner.

One way I help my clients is through what I call *Power Rehearsal for Crisis* (PRC). As their coach, I improvise dialogue and questions so that they can practice keeping their cool and thinking on their feet. This is a form of truly effective rehearsal.

Now it's your turn. How will you rehearse before any upcoming important situation?

4. Trustworthiness

Every day, we can build our opportunities for more success and personal fulfillment by doing what is necessary to fulfill our commitments. In so doing, we are appreciated as trustworthy. I hire people whom I trust. I devote my time and effort to loved ones, friends, clients and others whom I trust. Don't you?

How do we gain trust?
- Be a bit early for appointments.
- Do what you say you'll do.
- Be careful about your promises.
- Complete tasks a bit earlier than deadlines.
- Listen closely to other people. And let them know that you're paying full attention.

* * *

I invite you to take daily action along these lines:

L – listening

I – involved credibility

S – significant rehearsal
T – trustworthiness

To say it briefly, do what will make it easy for others to give you the One YES. You'll enjoy more opportunities. Your success will grow by Big Leaps.

* * * * * *

Topic #6
Book Two: Enlarge Your Life (Create More and Better in Your Life)
Secrets of the Hidden Side of Great Success

Do you really want success and fulfillment? Listen close: There is another side to success besides goal-achieving. To demonstrate confidence and strength, you need **the "3 Rs"— Rest, Recharge and Reconnect with Purpose.**

1. Rest
Sometimes, people restrict their interpretation of "rest" only to sleeping or sitting and doing nothing.

On the other hand, I'll add that it's helpful to consider resting different portions of your brain.

To write this article, I use one portion of my brain.

Later, I can rest by listening to music and assembling a jigsaw puzzle. At that point, I'm using another portion of my brain.

Let's go back to the conventional elements of sleep and "doing nothing." A friend once mentioned, "I make Sunday the one day when I do not have to do anything." That sounds like a good plan: making Sunday a true day of rest.

One morning as I was awakening a phrase came to mind: "To be strong is a choice."

To be strong includes resting and recharging. In order to function well and use all of your resources, you do need rest.

It's good to have regular "down time" in which you relax and experience being peaceful and calm.

What is "rest" to you?

How can you schedule rest for a portion of each day?

2. Recharge

We can look upon recharging as having some active element. For example, my sweetheart and I did helmet-diving—that's when you walk on the floor of the ocean. I was surprised to experience such a pressure difference only 28 feet down.

Having a bit of an adventure can feel like recharging. But recharging does not have to be adventurous. Just taking a 10 minute walk or talking for 5 minutes with a good friend on the phone can recharge your soul, mind and body. The idea of recharging is to create new energy for yourself.

What is "recharging" to you?

How will you schedule such activities?

3. Reconnect with Purpose

In my college level Designing Careers classes, I introduce students to one of my favorite questions to ask a successful person in an interview: "Knowing what you know now, what would you have done differently?"

A number of successful people I've talked with mention that they would have begun sooner to pursue a life of passion and purpose.

Here are a couple of a facets of a purpose:
- a) Who do you help?
- b) How do you express your unique creativity, talents and strengths?

c) Where is the joy?

This last question—*Where is the joy?*—is truly valuable. For example, I wrote a script for a short film. One purpose for doing the short film was to help a friend, "Sam," by providing footage for Sam's demonstration reel so that he could get more acting jobs. Then Sam dropped out due to his extreme work commitments.

Then I found myself asking, "Where is the joy?" I knew the script worked since I confirmed its viability with friends who are good screenwriters.

But with Sam out of the project, I found my interest drying up.

At this point, it's important to note: Just because you're good at something does not mean that you'll find joy and true purpose in it.

So I wrote a good script. But I did not like the characters enough to pursue it. So with Sam out of the picture, I dropped the project.

Now, it's your turn.

Answer these questions for yourself so you connect (or reconnect) with your personal purpose:

Who do you want to help?

How do you want to express yourself creatively?

Where is the joy?

* * *

When you want to feel successful and fulfilled, remember the other side beyond goal-achieving. Build yourself. Be strong when you use the *3 Rs—Rest, Recharge and Reconnect with Purpose.*

You'll enjoy life, and people will be glad to know you.

* * * * * *

Now, I'll share author Mike Robbins' insights so you'll enjoy your journey of enlarging your life. His article was originally written at the beginning of the new year, but it applies when we look at *this moment* as a new beginning.

New Year, Be You
by Mike Robbins

With the New Year still in its first few weeks, the annual "new year, new you" phenomenon is all around us – in the worlds of advertising, media, self-help and more. And while this time of year can be a great catalyst for positive change in our lives, what if we made a commitment to live our lives in the New Year focused on who we are, and not so much on what we do, what we accomplish, what we look like, what we're striving for, and more? One of best things we can do in this New Year is to focus on who we really are, instead of who we think we're supposed to be.

Who would we be without our accomplishments (or failures), our degrees (or lack thereof), our bank accounts, our experiences, our title, our home, our status, and more? As simple of a concept as this is for us to think about and discuss, at least on the surface, it's actually quite difficult for many of us, myself included, to genuinely separate who we are from what we do (or have done or not done). These past two years have taught many of us, in some cases quite painfully, how quickly the external circumstances of our lives can change dramatically and things can be taken away.

The deeper question for us to ponder here is really one of the big philosophical questions of life, "What makes me a valuable person?" While this is something we have all thought about to some degree, most of us don't really engage in this inquiry on a regular basis. And, when we do, we often think that if we just got more done, lost some weight, made more money, took a vacation, accomplished a goal, had more meaningful work, made it to retirement, or whatever, then we'd be "happier" or feel more "valuable." Sadly, as we've all experienced, this is not usually the case and is also one of the main reasons why most of our New Year's "resolutions" don't really last.

What if, in addition to having important goals, we could also expand our capacity for appreciating ourselves and being who we really are this year—having nothing to do with our external circumstances? What if just being ourselves, the way we are right now, is good enough?

Being ourselves fully, takes courage, commitment, and faith. It's a process of letting go of many false beliefs we've picked up from the collective consciousness—that we have to look good, be smart, know the right people, say the right things, have the proper experience, make a certain amount of money, and more, in order to be happy and successful in life. Being ourselves can be scary and counter intuitive, difficult and even off-putting, and, at times, lonely.

However, being our authentic self is liberating, exciting, and fulfilling. When we have the courage to just be who we are, without apology or pretence, so much of our suffering, stress, and worry in life simply goes away.

Here are a few things to consider and practice as you deepen your awareness of and capacity for being who you truly are in this New Year:

• **Tell the truth to yourself.** Think about and own how much of your self-worth is based on what you do, how you look, who you know, what you've accomplished, etc. (i.e. the external stuff). The more we let go of being defined by the external, the more freedom, peace, and power we can experience. And, as we really get honest with ourselves, we may realize that outside of these external things, we don't really know who we are. As scary as this may seem on the surface, it's actually great news and can give us access to a deeper and more meaningful experience of who we are.

- **Appreciate who you really are.** What do you appreciate about yourself that has nothing to do with anything external? In other words, what personal qualities (of being, not doing) do you value about yourself? The more we're able to tap into what we appreciate about who we are (not what we do), the more capacity we have for real confidence, peace, and self love.

- **Practice just being you.** As silly as it may sound, we all need to "practice" being ourselves. We have a great deal of experience being phony or being how we think we're supposed to be. It actually takes conscious practice for us to be able to just show up and be who we are. We can practice alone, with people we know, and with total strangers. This is all about awareness—paying attention to how we feel, what we're thinking, what we say, and how we show up. It's not about getting it right or doing anything specific, it's about letting go of our erroneous notions of how we think we're supposed to be, and just allowing ourselves to be who and how we are in the moment.

Have fun with this, talk to others about it, and have a lot of compassion with yourself as you practice—this is big stuff for most of us. This year, instead of trying to be a "new" you, just be yourself and see what happens.

How can you accept, appreciate, and simply BE yourself in the new year? What does this mean to you? What support do you need in your life this year to step more fully into who you really are?

Mike Robbins is the author of three books, *Focus on the Good Stuff and Be Yourself, Everyone Else is Already Taken,* and *Nothing Changes Until You Do.* As an expert in teamwork, emotional intelligence, and the powers of appreciation and authenticity, Mike delivers keynote addresses and customized seminars that empower people, teams, and organizations to work together effectively and be more successful. He has inspired tens of thousands of people around the world to reach new levels of awareness and productivity, both personally and professionally. Through his speeches, seminars, and writing, Mike teaches people important techniques that allow them to be more grateful, appreciative, and authentic with others and themselves.

His clients include Google, Wells Fargo, Adobe, Charles Schwab, Twitter, the U.S. Department of Labor, Gap, New York Life, Stanford University, Chevron, eBay, Kaiser, UC Berkeley, Genentech, the San Francisco Giants, and many others. Mike is a member of the National Speakers Association. He has been featured on ABC News, the Oprah radio network, in Forbes, the Washington Post, and many others. He is a regular contributor to Oprah.com and the Huffington Post. Mike had been drafted by the New York Yankees out of high school. He turned the Yankees down and instead chose to play baseball at Stanford University, where he pitched in the College World Series. Mike was drafted by the Kansas City Royals out of Stanford and played three seasons of professional baseball with the Royals organization before arm injuries ended his playing career while still in the minor leagues.

In addition to earning a degree from Stanford in American Studies with a specialization in race and ethnicity, Mike has extensively studied many disciplines of both personal and professional development, and received training from the Coaches Training Institute.

Mike is a former board member for two non-profit organizations—Challenge Day (a powerful youth organization that focuses on peace, healing, and personal development for teens) and The Peace Alliance (which includes a grassroots political campaign to create a cabinet level U.S. Department of Peace).

In addition to his three books, Mike is also a contributing author to: *Chicken Soup for the Single Parent's Soul, Creating a Marriage You'll Love,* and *Thirty Things to Do When You Turn Thirty.*

Reach Mike at www.mike-robbins.com

* * *

Mike Robbins reminds us that an enlarged life is not just about more accomplishments. It's about how "you accept, appreciate, and simply BE yourself."

* * * * * *

Now, I'll share Dr. Martin Crous' insights about decluttering your thoughts and improving self-confidence.

How to De-clutter Your Life and Improve Your Confidence
by Martin Crous, Ph.D.

Many people carry around with them a lot of "baggage" or "clutter" in their minds.

When I say this I mean that they are still holding onto things that they say they should do but don't; the person who they had a row with but both are not speaking to each other—but both want to; the coulds and shoulds in your life that hold you back—you need to let go, but you don't.

These people carry around with them a lot of emotional attention that they could be doing without and focusing on something more productive instead!

Are you like this?

If you are, I bet it had a negative influence on your confidence and self-esteem.

The approach

Take a look at your life and get rid of this baggage by asking yourself a series of questions and by completing the following exercise.

In effect, what we are doing is making certain tasks "complete", drawing a line under them and moving on.

Another term for this is "psychological completion" or just "completion."

The following set of questions can be taken at one sitting or over a number of hours/days.

By writing the answers down they become more formal.

Get to it and watch your confidence soar!

1. **Putting up with!**

   • Make a list of 10 things that you are putting up with at home.
   • Make a list of 10 things that you are putting up with at work.
   • Make a list of 10 things that you are putting up with in any other area of your life.
   • Make an action plan to get rid of/communicate these things that you have been putting up with.

2. **Unfinished matters!**

   • Make a list of things that are unresolved/unfinished in your life.
   • Make an action plan of how to reduce this number!
   • Do you need to clear the air with anyone? If so, just do it! Life is too short!
   • Did you ever say that you were going to call someone or keep in touch with someone yet have done nothing about it? If yes, call them or send an email to them today.
   • Let go of as many coulds, woulds, shoulds, maybes, oughts as you can. Write these down.

3. **Your standards!**

   • Write down the standards that you have been saying to yourself that you should have; let go of these and write down a list of the standards that you are going to have in your life from this day forward.
   • List 5 people who you admire the most. Identify their greatest qualities, behavior and how they lead their life. What standards do they have? What standards could you

raise starting today to be more like them?

• Respect that others' standards will be different from your own. Think of 5 close colleagues or friends—what are their standards and how are they different to yours?

By completing these exercises you will be able to focus more on the here, the now and the future.

You will now be able to let go of some of the things that have been taking up your valuable attention units—those things that knock your self esteem.

Dr. Martin Crous dedicates his life in helping people discover and put into action the tools, strategies, and resources that create amazing results and personal fulfillment. His travels have taken him all over the world, and he has coached, consulted and trained with everything from new start-ups to multi-million dollar companies, showing them how to massively grow their business, increase their profits and achieve all their goals and dreams. He is an International Accredited and Certified Professional NLP Master Practitioner, Success Coach, Consultant, Mentor, Professional International Speaker, Published Author and has coached people all over the world face to face or on the phone.

Website: http://www.martincrous.com
Twitter: #MartinCrousPhD

* * *

Dr. Martin Crous provided the means to clarify how you want to move forward from this day forward.

* * * * * *

Now, I'll share Patricia Fripp's methods for focusing on the crucial and simple steps to enhancing your career. When you focus these steps you clear your mind of mental clutter.

7 Fripp Do's – How to Present to Senior Management Without Being Terrified
by Patricia Fripp, CSP, CPAE

It's no secret… the higher up the corporate ladder you go, the more important your public speaking skills become. To position yourself for promotion and career success you need to learn what it takes to sell yourself and your ideas to senior management. That requires learning high-level public speaking skills to become a confident, competent communicator. Here are seven public speaking tips to help you get started.

Seven Fripp Do's

1. Practice. A report to senior managers is not a conversation; however, it must sound conversational. Once you have your notes, practice by speaking out loud to an associate, or when you are driving to work, or on the treadmill. Make sure you are familiar with what you intend to say. It is not about being perfect. It is about being personable. (Remember, rehearsal is the work; performance is the relaxation.)

2. Open with your conclusions. Don't make your senior-level audience wait to find out why you are there.

3. Describe the benefits if your recommendation is adopted. Make these benefits seem vivid and obtainable.

4. Describe the costs, but frame them in a positive manner. If possible, show how not following your recommendation will cost even more….

5. List your specific recommendations, and keep your presentation on target. Wandering generalities will lose their interest. You must focus on the bottom line. Report on the deals, not the details.

6. Look everyone in the eye when you talk. You will be more persuasive and believable. (You can't do this if you are reading!)

7. Be brief. The fewer words you can use to get your message across, the better. Jerry Seinfeld says, "I spend an hour taking an eight-word sentence and making it five." That's because he knows it would be funnier. In your case, shorter is more memorable and repeatable.

* * *

6 Mistakes Sales Professionals Make in Their Sales Presentations
by Patricia Fripp, CSP, CPAE

You have a competitive edge when your sales presentations are more powerfully persuasive in your than your competition's.

- Are you losing sales you feel you deserve to make?

- Would it be helpful if your prospect remembered what you said?

- Would it be beneficial if three weeks later, your prospect could repeat your key ideas?

- Would it be profitable if your prospect vividly knew why others selected you as their vendor of choice?

Are you making one or all of the most common, biggest mistakes made by sales professionals?

- **Thanking prospects for their time** instead of thanking them for the opportunity to discuss doing business.

- **Using a flawed conversation or speech structure. Focusing on your own company history** instead of focusing on how you can discover or solve the client's problems.

- **Talking about what you do** rather than telling stories of satisfied clients and painting a picture of how this client's condition will be improved with your product or service.

- **Speaking at the wrong level of abstraction.** Being too technical or too vague.

- **Starting with a weak, predictable opening** and not closing on a memorable conclusion.

- **Thinking the PowerPoint is the presentation.** Technology can be used effectively to support your message, but should never be used as a crutch.

Patricia Fripp, CSP, CPAE works with organizations and individuals who want to put their best foot forward by gaining powerful, persuasive, presentation skills. She is a Hall of Fame Keynote Speaker, Executive Speech Coach, and Sales Presentation Skills Expert.
 (415)753-6556, Fax (415)753-0914
 PFripp@ix.netcom.com, www.fripp.com
 www.fripp.com/blog/ twitter@Pfripp

* * *

Patricia Fripp reminds us that the path to success involves practicing simple but vital methods.

* * * * * *

Conclusion to Book Two

In Book Two, we covered a number of methods that you can use to enlarge your life. Now, in Book 3, we'll cover how you can maintain your enhanced lifestyle. It helps for you to *nurture yourself.*

BOOK THREE:
NURTURE YOURSELF
(ENLARGE YOUR LIFE)

Have you ever added something to your life and felt a feeling of overwhelm press upon you? It helps to use strategies for *nurturing yourself*.

I invite you to study and practice the following methods covered in the four topics below:

Topics:
1) Rescue Yourself from Feeling "Blah"
2) How You Can Overcome "Successful But Stuck"
3) How to Feel Better and Speed Up Success
4) Really Succeed: How You Can Handle Burnout and Keep Going

Topic #1
Book Three: Nurture Yourself (Enlarge Your Life)
Rescue Yourself from Feeling "Blah"

Do you have goals but sometimes feel exhausted? It's strange how friends may say, "Well, you've chosen to have those goals"—as if that guards you from exhaustion. We know that anyone can get tired. The scary part is when one's goals do not feel as exciting anymore. We'll use the A.I.M. process:
A – amaze yourself in advance
I – increase renewal
M – measure progress

1. Amaze yourself in advance
Many of us begin with a goal and a picture of how much better our life will be upon accomplishing it.

Then painful reality sets in. If you're dropping twenty pounds, the first four may slide off pretty quickly. But then you might hit a wall. And worse yet, the goal of feeling slimmer may fade in intensity.

I suggest that you find some way to experience the "good part" now.

For example, when one is slimmer, it's easier to move.

Instead of pushing yourself with another run, perhaps, have a walk and enjoy simply walking. This is like a glimpse of further good experiences.

When I say, "amaze yourself in advance," I'm talking about having some form of experience in the present moment that gives your an in-the-moment feeling of the good you expect to experience when the goal is accomplished.

For example, when I envisioned completing my first

feature film, I had the clear picture of audience members laughing at the appropriate comedic moments of the film.

During rehearsals, I enjoyed when certain lines got the cast and crew to laugh—that, for me, was part of "amazing myself in advance."

Now it's your turn.

How can you experience, on a small scale, a preview of the good feelings you'll enjoy when you accomplish your goal?

2. Increase renewal

I've completed many projects (feature film, graphic novel, 22 books, audio novel, speaking at Stanford University, and more). *And,* I have felt really tired on the road to getting something finished.

Then there are times when something in my personal life knocks me down. In 1995, I suffered through the breakup of a nearly eight year relationship. It hurt deeply.

Even worse—I felt numbed to anything that might feel good.

Finally, I was surprised by what reinvigorated me. It was ...wait for it...seeing Disney's 1995 feature film *Pocahontas* at the movie theater.

Music, humor, romance and expressions of love reached my heart.

And I admit it: I cried during the song "Colors of the Wind."

The film *Pocahontas* was an important part of my renewal.

On New Year's Day, I went to the movie theater and saw the Disney feature film *Frozen*.

During the song, "Let It Go," Elsa, the Snow Queen, finally gets away from other people and gives full expression to her special powers. She builds a castle made of ice. She is finally clear and defiant in expressing herself. She sings, "Here I stand and here I'll stay!"

The big thing for me is that during the film I experienced a catharsis. Also, I experienced how art can invigorate us. I am re-energized to continue moving forward with my team on the graphic novel I've written: *Jack AngelSword*.

I am an artist who has been re-energized by the work of other artists.

Now, I ask you:

How can you experience the work of someone that will energize you in your own path?

(For example, writers read the good work of other writers.)

3. Measure progress

The truth I've learned is that outside of getting coached in athletics, many of us do not receive the "Good job! Well done!" comments we crave.

I invite you to write your own log of your good efforts and successes each day. In this way, you'll be your own coach praising you.

For many years, I've introduced my clients to the value of something I use: a *Daily Journal of Victories and Blessings*. Your "blessings" entries can be as simple as "I'm grateful for the surprise phone call from my friend Lynsey." You can also note the bigger things like hearing that your family member came through surgery with a great prognosis. Victories can include going for your daily walk or completing an exercise session.

According to research studies, it turns out that people who experience more joy are those who have daily "gratitude practices."

For example, sometimes, as I walk to the building where I teach college students, I have an internal "chant": I am grateful for my life. I am grateful for my students. I am grateful for this college . . .

Now it's your turn:

Pull out your journal and write (and say aloud):

I am grateful for . . .

* * *

Please consider that if you feel tired in heart or spirit, this feeling can pass.

Find ways to experience art and good sides of life.

In this way, you clear a path so you can have renewal arrive in your life.

Every step in this direction is truly worth it.

* * * * * *

Topic #2
Book Three: Nurture Yourself (Enlarge Your Life)
How You Can Overcome "Successful But Stuck"

Do you feel stuck? To some of us, it's surprising to observe that we actually feel stuck when we're successful, at least by other people's external standards.

Now, we'll use the H.E.A.R. process.

H – heed your inner voice
E – engage
A – appeal to joy for your new chapter
R – reinvest

1. Heed your Inner Voice

Are there a bunch of people who think they have answers for what you "should be doing"? Some say, "Slow down." Others say, "Speed up—you're not living up to your potential."

Some say, "Put aside your artistic endeavors."

Really? What crystal ball do they have?!

Instead, consider that it's an "AND" world. You can pursue your art AND work a job that pays the bills.

Heed Your Inner Voice. Not someone else's voice of fear.

Instead, listen for your voice of intuition.

Here's the difference:

Voice of Fear: contract, hide, avoid taking risks.

Voice of Intuition: expand, experiment, take appropriate risks.

To heed your inner voice, you need to make time and space so you can listen to it.

As people offer you advice (much of it unasked for), simply respond, "Thanks for your concern. I appreciate it. I'll really consider what you've shared with me."

I call this process: Getting *thinkspace*. Avoid agreeing to advice too quickly. Instead, use the above response to create thinkspace so that you can heed your inner and true voice.

2. Engage

Try new things. Several years ago, I submitted my headshot (photograph) to be a model for a software company's website. When I arrived on set, the photographer said, "Oh, you're Asian, but you were born and raised in America. They move in a different way."

Now I was afraid that I would lose the job. I had already spent money to get to the location.

"Yes," I replied, "And how about I change my posture?"

So I changed my posture and placed my hands together in ways I've seen Asian Buddhists monks do.

"That works," the photographer said. He framed the shot with my "praying hands" not visible.

By saying yes to this opportunity and adapting, I earned my first $400-in-one-hour.

How about you? What appropriate risks could you take? How can you engage in life in new ways?

3. Appeal to joy for your new chapter

I'll ask again: Do you feel stuck?

Consider that you're about to enter a new chapter of life.

What do you want this new chapter to include?

I'll give you a secret: Identify something that will give you the experience of joy.

Pause for a moment. Picture what you enjoy doing. How can you incorporate what you enjoy in the new chapter of your life?

Success is not the key to happiness. Happiness is the key to success. If you love what you are doing, you will be successful.
– Albert Schweitzer

4. Reinvest

First, let's realize that many of us are invested in certain stories we tell ourselves. Some stories are helpful like: "I'm good at talking with people."

Other stories can hold us back like: "I'm just so awkward at networking events."

I invite you to reinvest in yourself. If you feel that you have some impediment to rising to your next level of success, get some coaching. You can use books, audio programs and workshops to raise the level of your game. [And I applaud that you're reading this book.]

On the other hand, I've been sad when listening to some individuals who have given up on their education. That is, those people who say, "Oh, I'm done with that. I attended college and that's enough."

Instead, the top successful people I have interviewed, all share a particular trait: They purposely expand their knowledge and skills every year.

This is the road to success and fulfillment.

* * * * * *

Topic #3
Book Three: Nurture Yourself (Enlarge Your Life)
How to Feel Better and Speed Up Success

Have you had a big disappointment and you want to feel strong again? You can use your mind to move forward faster. We'll focus on the M.I.N.D. process:

M – move from complain to adapt quickly
I – invite thoughts of "I'm in a new chapter now."
N – notice "That was a good run."
D – drop demands and welcome preferences
1. Move from complain to adapt quickly

Do you know someone who uses up a lot of time complaining about things that have changed?

Have you noticed how a complainer drains the life out of a room?

Merely complaining keeps you stuck. When you switch to adapting, you place yourself in the driver's seat.

When you find yourself complaining, ask yourself: "How can I adapt to this situation? How can I find some lesson here and improve what I do for the next time?"

For example, many years ago, I was invited to train an audience in how to make products: audio programs and books. During the speech, I stood up and quickly diagramed on a whiteboard these details:

- Record a speech (there's your audio product).
- Transcribe the speech and add questions (there's your workbook).
- Combine a few speeches (there's your first short book).

After the speech, I received a couple of emails that had complaints in them. This bothered me a lot. I even complained to a family member: "Why couldn't they take in the value I was sharing?"

That's when I applied these questions: *"How can I adapt to this situation? How can I find some lesson here and improve what I do for the next time?"*

Upon reflection, I realized that I had missed an important thing that the audience wanted. They *asked* for methods to make products. *But what they needed and wanted* was for me to hold their hand and say, "If you've hesitated and felt any fear about making your first product, I'm right there with you. For my first speech and my first book, I was terrified. Let's talk about how you can flow forward while nurturing yourself and facing your real and understandable fear . . ."

I also learned (and adapted) to sit down on a stool during portions of my speech. When I sit down, I slow down and I share heartfelt moments with the audience.

You can see that *there is real power in adapting.*

2. Invite thoughts of "I'm in a new chapter now."

Sometimes life hits us really hard. When a close friend committed suicide, I felt knocked to the floor. I'd wake up and think about calling him—but he was gone. I even recorded his outgoing voicemail message in a effort to stop him from disappearing from my life.

But I had to reconcile that I was in a new chapter of life. My deceased friend belonged to the previous chapter of my life.

The same thing hits me during the holiday season. In the last five years, I have not had a positive Christmas day with my father. It seems he's gotten more bitter each year.

I long for a positive time with my father during the holidays. So far it has not happened. So I reconcile myself to: "I'm in a new chapter now."

I'm in a new chapter of life. It will never be the same. But it can be good—just different.

So I invite you make yourself aware of what is good in your present life.

Minimize longing for the past. Remind yourself with "I'm in a new chapter now."

3. Notice "That was a good run."

"Cheryl," one of the teachers I know has had her schedule shifted around. She no longer teaches her favorite class. This troubles her deeply.

In a recent conversation, she let me know that she wanted to move on and not ruminate about her loss. I suggested a phrase that helps me turn my thoughts and feelings to gratitude: "That was a good run."

We can realize that we miss something now because it had been a good part of our lives. It was part of a previous chapter in our lives. Aren't you glad you had that good thing in your life for a time?

Remind yourself by using the phrase: "That was a good run."

Cheryl finally said, "I had that class for six years. That was a good run."

4. Drop demands and welcome preferences

Want to feel better? Consider this process: drop demands that the world be different than it is. In essence, you do not *demand* people do something (we do not control them). But you do acknowledge your have *preferences* for how things might go.

For example, I mentioned earlier that my father is highly negative and makes family members deeply upset during the holiday season.

Instead of fretting about his attitude, I realize that his attitude is his own responsibility. I summarize the situation as: "It is what it is."

I avoid trying to demand that he act in a different manner. I certainly have no control over his actions or attitude.

What I can do is minimize my interactions with him and speak up when he says something demeaning. My truthful observations do not change his behavior. It is simply a matter of my "speaking my own truth." Sometimes, that has to be enough. "It is what it is."

"It is what it is" frees me up to avoid ruminating about my sadness about my father. I shift to doing something else like being kind to others and taking action to welcome opportunities. In this way, I'm not stuck in the past (even if it is an upset that happened 10 minutes ago). I move forward.

* * *

In summary, here are the useful phrases, you might consider memorizing:
- I'm in a new chapter now.
- I'm grateful for that previous chapter.
- That was a good run.
- It is what it is.

You can use your mind to be flexible. You're better able to jump at opportunities for success when you avoid being lost in complaints and past memories.

Stay in the present moment. Then move forward with greater ease and success.

* * * * * *

Topic #4
Book Three: Nurture Yourself (Enlarge Your Life)

Really Succeed: How You Can Handle Burnout and Keep Going

Have you felt some form of burnout? When you want to experience success, you can count on times when you expend great energy and then need to recover. You may feel worn out—so use the S.A.L.V.E. process to sooth any "wounds" you may feel:

S – save space
A – arrange rotation
L – learn something new
V – value new surroundings
E – enjoy something

1. Save space

Is there space in your schedule just devoted to nurturing you?

So often, I hear people almost bragging about how busy they are. Is this really something to brag about? No. Here's why: by exclaiming how busy you are you are actually increasing your stress.

[As a sidenote: This section is about what we might call "mild burnout" or "non-clinical burnout" as a number of individuals mention in daily conversations. On the other hand, a more severe form of burnout has been studied and measured with The Maslach Burnout Inventory that uses a three-dimensional description of exhaustion, cynicism, and inefficacy. It is reported that severe burnout requires therapy and often a career change. Such severe burnout is beyond the scope of this section.]

Best-selling author Richard Carlson (*Don't Sweat the Small Stuff*) revealed a secret to me. He said that another author told him that even if you are scheduled to speak in 12 cities in 10 days, you still only do one thing at a time. What this means is: your schedule may be full but you can assure yourself that it is only one thing after another.

Further, you can assure yourself that you will rest when you can. While you're seated waiting for your next flight, you can do some deep breathing (also known as belly breathing). This rest is something that is nurturing to you.

Now I invite you to literally schedule time for yourself. What can you do that will empower you? A ten minute walk? An uplifting phone call with a positive friend? Listening to music? Petting your cat or dog? Pick something and do it and feel refreshed.

2. Arrange rotation

Are you simply tired of doing the same thing day in and day out? Could you somehow rotate your activities?

I find it wonderfully invigorating to rotate from working on my graphic novel *Jack AngelSword* to a short film I'm producing to non-fiction writing.

More importantly, rotating your activities can save you from the "hamster wheel" in life. Some people get stuck trying to do more and more of the same thing but receiving less and less benefit. A workaholic may work harder and devote more time but feel less whole and healthy. This is like any form of addiction. The same amount of the drug gives diminished pleasure.

Fortunately, the solution is to rotate to doing something different. If you do not find a certain activity to be fun or relaxing anymore, try something new and different.

3. Learn something new

Some people take a cooking class and it brightens their whole week. I know someone who started taking yoga classes and the yoga class became her oasis in the middle of the week.

A big benefit of learning something new is feeling certain types of thrills: "Oh! I can do this now!" or "Oooh—how interesting!"

Now, it's your turn. What can you do to bring new learning into your life?

4. Value new surroundings

Simply driving to a nearby city, and walking around might give you a boost in positive feelings. Recently, I talked with a dear friend who told me that she goes to museums to "fill her up" with new inspiration and energy.

How can you go someplace new? You could simply travel in a new way to work. Perhaps, you could stop by a park that you normally pass when you run errands.

Research shows that you do not have to have an extended time in the new place. The idea is to have some time—even 15 minutes or 30 minutes—in new surroundings.

5. Enjoy something

During my speeches, I often mention what I call *Top Six Targets*. This is a method of noting in about 2 minutes your top six goals for the next day. If you do these six items, you'll have a good, productive day. I suggest: 2 for you, 2 for family and 2 for work.

When you think about 2 for you, consider something fun or relaxing for yourself, that is under your own control. For example, every day, I see something that inspires me to laugh (such as a video or film clip on YouTube). Some people call laughter "inner jogging." I know that a few minutes of laughter provide a bright moment in my day.

Everyday, I also listen to empowering music.

What would you like to try so that you can experience some enjoyment today?

* * *

Burnout is a critical issue for all of us coping with packed schedules and intense stress. The solution is to become "stress-skilled" or to become "a personal recovery expert for yourself."

Use the guidelines of S.A.L.V.E. so that you become a resilient person.

* * * * * *

Conclusion to Book Three

In Book Three, we explored methods so that you nurture yourself. You need to constantly renew yourself so you have the resources to maintain your new, "enlarged lifestyle."

Next, in *Book Four*, you'll learn methods to enjoy life's many facets including: happiness, financial abundance, loving relationships—and feeling soulfully fulfilled.

BOOK FOUR: ENJOY LIFE'S MANY FACETS (HAPPINESS, FINANCIAL ABUNDANCE, LOVING RELATIONSHIPS AND FEELING SOULFULLY FULFILLED)

In various conversations with clients and others, I notice that beneath all the striving for success there is a supposition that "success brings happiness."

I always remember this quote:

Success is not the key to happiness. Happiness is the key to success. If you love what you are doing, you will be successful.
 - Albert Schweitzer

To help you develop more happiness and reserves in your life, we'll now explore these topics:

1) How You Can Experience Real Freedom and Joy
2) Discover the Hidden Side—Secrets of Riches and Romance

3) Protect Your Relationships (How to Handle Anger)
4) Untangle Yourself from the Ego-self and Then Support Your Relationship
5) How You Can Make the Crucial Difference (The Power of Listening)
6) Soulful Time Management
7) Replace Fear with Love
8) Get More Done—Faster and Better for True Success

Topic #1
Book Four: Enjoy Life's Many Facets

How You Can Experience Real Freedom And Joy

Would you like to enjoy more moments of happiness?

To experience a real, positive shift in how you experience your day-to-day living, let's focus on two premises.
- A thought precedes a feeling.
- You're only one thought away from happiness, courage or love.

Here is a pragmatic example. Teresa, a person I know, recently had to move out for a few days with her family. Why? Their building was being tented so that it would be engulfed in a gas to free the building from termites.

Teresa's first thought emphasized how stressful this whole ordeal was to her. So much inconvenience. Some things would need to be double-bagged, and others would need to be dragged to the hotel. She even felt physically ill.

So the temporary move could be called a problem, hassle or "waste of time."

I suggested this idea: "Oh, you're having a mini-vacation."

Think of it. A vacation involves many of the same things.

- packing
- eating at restaurants
- sleeping at a hotel
- having time away from one's usual routines

So what do you think? If you must face a certain event, what would be more empowering? What would simply feel better? What thought would help you? Can you make a personal choice and label the experience as something that you can use?

Finally, let's look at a certain pattern: "Yes, but…" I asked Teresa, "So you enjoyed your first dinner at the restaurant." She replied, "Yes. It was at one of my favorite restaurants, but the sirloin was not tender."

The rest of the conversation demonstrated that the one detail—the not tender meat—colored her whole experience. She didn't mention that the family was together and enjoyed laughter. The dessert was delicious. And the sirloin even tasted good!

Do you see how one thought creates her final experience of an event?

One thought becomes the whole story she tells herself and others over and over again.

On the other hand, *your real freedom manifests in how you direct your focus.*

Your first thought may be one that lowers your mood.

Now, you have a choice about your NEXT thought.

We're not talking about "controlling your thoughts."

Instead picture the opportunity to direct your focus on something that empowers you. I use the metaphor of a flashlight. **Direct the "flashlight of your focus" to something good.** Light up the idea that makes you feel better.

For example, here's an empowering thought: "To

experience happy moments, you do NOT need to be free of every problem or inconvenience."

You can do two things. You can focus on the thought: "I am happy right now." And then you can take it up another step. Use an Afformation (devised by author Noah St. John). An Afformation is an empowering question. In this case, you can ask, "Why am I happy right now?"

Then, write down your thoughts that follow the word "because."

- Because my loved ones are well
- Because I'm enjoying _____
- Because I'm free of _____
- Because I'm focusing on _____

Remember, to experience freedom and joy, direct your focus—that is, pick where you focus your "flashlight of attention."

Happiness often is one thought away.

* * * * * *

Along the line that happiness is one thought away, here are 50 thoughts about "how to live rich" from top author and millionaire Randy Gage.

50 Secrets of Prosperity
by Randy Gage

If you've been following my Twitter feed since I got back online, then you know that I've been sharing 50 secrets about prosperity. A lot of you have asked me to compile them in one spot. Here they are.

Some are whimsical; others are profound. Some are obvious; others may surprise you. Some make you feel good; others may make you mad. But each one highlights a certain truth about prosperity, and what it takes to live a prosperous and abundant life.

1) Rich people think differently than broke people.

2) Healthy people think differently than sick people.

3) Happy people think differently than depressed people.

4) You're not poor because you don't have money. You're poor if you don't have a dream.

5) Governments do not create prosperity. At best, they facilitate it. Usually, they squander it.

6) Money at its very essence is energy – which can be attracted or repelled.

7) With a powerful vision that pulls you toward it – you bend the universe to your will.

8) When your dream is bold enough, the facts no longer matter.

9) Your past does not have to determine your future. But only when you decide to break the cycle.

10) You can watch five to six hours of television a day, or you can be rich, but you can't do both.

11) You can be a victim or a victor, but you can't be both.

12) Poverty is not the absence of money and material things; it is a mindset.

13) Prosperity is not an abundance of money and material things; it is a mindset.

14) You might think you have a money shortage, but it's really only an idea shortage.

15) Never let anyone else's limiting belief become yours.

16) If you want to become wealthy, stop taking financial advice from broke people.

17) Your wealth grows exactly at the same rate your prosperity consciousness does.

18) The only free cheese is in the mousetrap.

19) Wealth is created by adding value and solving problems.

20) You must be willing to let go of who you have been, to become who you are meant to be.

21) Prosperity is your birthright and natural condition.

22) The universe can only do for you what it can do through you.

23) Gossiping about others creates a negative prosperity debt.

24) You must be willing to give up some things you want, to get the things you really want.

25) If you don't invest in yourself, it's probably a pretty bad investment for anyone else.

26) Only argue for the limitations you really want to keep!

27) Only acknowledge your limitations for the purpose of overcoming them.

28) To embolden yourself, surround yourself with bold people.

29) Money doesn't buy happiness. But neither does poverty.

30) Bills are simply invoices for blessings you've already received. Treat them accordingly.

31) Surround yourself with people who dream bigger than you do.

32) You can't out give the universe.

33) The best thing you can do for the poor, hungry and exploited is not be one of them.

34) When you get negative people out of your life, negative things happen a lot less frequently.

35) Vengeance must walk out before love can walk in.

36) The universe won't give you your next assignment until you're overqualified for your current one.

37) Let go of the need to be liked. Successful people threaten mediocrity.

38) Haters don't hate you. They hate themselves because they don't have the guts to do what you're doing.

39) Salesy is always better than brokey.

40) Never shop anywhere women are wearing curlers in their hair.

41) Build your own dream instead of borrowing the dreams of others.

42) Build a dream so compelling it pulls you towards it.

43) Your dream needs to be as big as you are. And that's really big.

44) If you're not scared, you need a bigger goal.

45) When you make your dream bigger, it makes you bigger.

46) If you find yourself starting over too much, stop giving up so easily.

47) To unleash your power, start believing in your power.

48) If your dream isn't outrageous, you're just not being realistic.

49) Treat the people you meet today as if they will be gone tomorrow.

50) Make sure you die with more memories than dreams.

If you find these insights helpful, you may want to bookmark or favorite this page [on his website]. Please share this post with the people in your world. And as always, live rich!

Randy Gage is the author of nine books, including the New York Times bestseller, *Risky Is the New Safe*. He has spoken in 48 U.S. States, all Canadian provinces and 48 other countries, to more than 2 million people. He was listed in the "Who's Hot" article for Speaker Magazine and in 2013 was inducted into the Speakers Hall of Fame.
   www.RandyGage.com
   Prosperity TV at http://www.youtube.com/randygage

* * *

A number of prosperous authors and business people mention that money does not insure happiness. However, an empowered approach to creating wealth (as mentioned above by Randy Gage) can be helpful to bring you more happy moments.
   Research implies that relationships are a primary source of happiness. And now we'll continue with Topic #2 that addresses relationships.

Topic #2
Book Four: Enjoy Life's Many Facets
Discover the Hidden Side—Secrets of Riches and Romance

Did you know that there's a Hidden Side to riches and romance in your love relationship? What if you really could increase your good, warm, and romantic feelings? How about increasing your prosperity and dropping your money worries?

Finally, here I get to share what my mentors have taught me and what I've learned through hard experience.

Several studies demonstrate that money conflicts are a primary stressor that often leads to divorce. So it's best to learn the methods of Prosperous Couples, found in this article.

Perhaps, you've asked:
Can my relationship get better than this?
Can we ever stop having horrible conflict over money?
The answers are yes and yes.

I know from personal experience. My sweetheart and I are stronger and closer now in our 14 years together.

2 Secrets of the Hidden Side of Romance and Riches
First, why do I call it the "Hidden Side"?

Because our first thoughts may be the "obvious version of romance"—that is, our partner does something nice for us. One of my clients, Stephen, mentioned how delighted his new girlfriend Judy was when he was kind to her. Judy said with zeal to her best friend, "He gave me an awesome foot massage!" Imagine if Judy were completely exhausted and burned out by her job. Would she have had such a delighted experience while with Stephen? Maybe. You see, the Hidden

Side of Riches and Romance is really about *how you are functioning* in the relationship. This is a truly different thought than: "We would have a good relationship is he would just change!"

Secret #1: You often experience your thought and not the other person.

At first, this may seem like a strange idea. However, your feelings can change on a dime based on one thought.

Picture your best memory from childhood. Probably you had a delightful surprise, or someone really demonstrated their love and care for you.

Now, recall a big mistake you made at your current job or a previous position. That memory likely brings up a bad feeling.

Notice that in both of the above experiences: a thought precedes a feeling.

As I mentioned: Secret #1: You often experience your thought and not the other person.

If Serena says, "Joe is a romantic soul," she looks for all the times that he has done something she deems romantic.

However, if Serena holds a different thought in mind, "Joe just lives in his head," she looks for all her disappointments in which Joe was trying to use logic and talk her out of her feelings.

It's one thought at a given moment. And then she's not experiencing the "wholeness that is Joe." She experiences her thought and NOT Joe as a person.

Here's another common thought: "You're not romantic, anymore."

That's NOT a neutral thought. It's actually a form of attack. A man hears this, and he feels threatened. Now, he feels like he's been called "less than" his earlier self.

The unfortunate truth is that many boys grow up feeling that they're in a never-ending, never-resting competition.

I'll say it plainly: Avoid triggering a man's competitive "mental baggage."

Here's what helps. Point to a successful effort that the man did and express appreciation.

Before You Say Something Out Loud, Internally Challenge the Thought.

Wait a moment. Ask yourself, "Is this thought—'You're not romantic, anymore'—really true?"

What if Joe still opens doors for Serena? That's romantic.

It would be great if Serena could appreciate and demonstrate her appreciation for the kindness of Joe's opening the door for her.

Method A: Act as a Graceful Receiver

So we start with expressing appreciation for what Joe already does.

Still, Serena misses the surprise gifts, such as roses.

How can she INSPIRE Joe to give her roses again?

The solution is for Serena to act as Graceful Receiver. Serena can say, "Hey, I want to thank you again for when you gave me surprises—you know like roses. That made me feel good."

Serena notices Joe frown a bit. She could add, "Hey, one rose works, too."

As a Graceful Receiver, Serena does two things:

a) She expresses appreciation

b) She demonstrates that she's NOT holding out for something expensive (perhaps, even beyond the couple's budget).

[For more about enhancing romance and riches in your relationship, see my book *Wake Up Your Spirit to Prosperity: Experience More Love and Prosperity with Your Mate*.]

Secret #2: For you to experience true romance, riches, and love, you need to act with inner strength and the essence of love.

Many of us are so caught up in goals and doing, that we have no energy left for our mate or even creating financial abundance. Many of us struggle to protect our current job. (You may have heard of the expression: "J.O.B.– just over broke.")

Here's another trap: When many of us think about riches, we get caught up in standard thoughts about "achieving success" and "going for your goals."

Many of us look to something good happening "on the outside." Only when something works on the outside, do many of us feel prosperous.

Instead, let's look "on the inside."

I'm talking about becoming a **Graceful Giver.** This is beyond "going for your goals" or "achieving success." Instead, it is an *in-the-present-moment* Mindset.

Imagine this: at your core essence, you are love. You are part of the Divine. We note that a number of spiritual texts express: "God is love." Numerous spiritual paths suggest that there is a divine spark in each human being.

So you do *not* have to search for love. Instead, act from your essence. You are love. Another way to look at this is to act as a Graceful Giver.

Graceful Givers give attention and focus because that is simply an expression of who they are.

They shift their attention away from what they can get by

doing an action and instead put their focus on being loving in this moment.

Simply being present with another person is such a gift to him or her.

When I suggest "being present," I mean focusing your attention on that person's joy or pain.

It takes energy and strength. Do what's necessary to keep yourself calm and strong. Sleep enough. Eat with your focus on good nutrition. Devote time to people who uplift you.

And shift your thoughts from actions being simply a transaction: the old idea of "you do good to receive good."

Instead focus on being a Graceful Giver, who is kind. You're kind because that is your essence—not because you're counting on good things to happen "as a reward."

Several years ago, I knew someone, "Matthew," who told me that he was angry with God. Why? He said that he did everything right: said the right prayers, attended the right events, and abstained from certain activities. And he expected to be compensated!

When things did not turn out in the way he wanted, Matthew was upset. He did not pause and think: "Perhaps, I need to learn something here. Maybe, I'll learn something, and that will prepare me to be helpful to others at some time in the future."

On the other hand, I had a different experience. Many years ago, I worked for three different banks. The jobs had nothing to do with my best talents, so I was glad to move on. But my past experiences in corporate America have still proved useful. They now serve my college students in my Designing Careers classes.

Method B: Act as a Graceful Giver

You can act as a Graceful Giver by asking, *"How can I be supportive of what you're doing?"*

You may not always find a match to fulfill the request in exactly the way the person envisions it. But you can help in some way. For example, my client Cindy helped her friend, an author, by tweeting about her friend's new book. Cindy did not post a comment on Facebook because she felt that the book was not a match for her Facebook circle of contacts. But Cindy did find a way to be helpful. She was still a Graceful Giver.

Finally, to be a Graceful Giver, avoid being a bitter martyr like "Matthew." Don't give to get a reward. Give simply because that's what you do. And avoid trying to keep score.

Again, remember:

You do NOT have to look for love; instead love IS your essence.

When you radiate love, the universe naturally brings you more opportunities for prosperity and loving-kindness in return.

* * * * * *

Topic #3
Book Four: Enjoy Life's Many Facets

Protect Your Relationships (How to Handle Anger)

People watch how one handles anger. Can you trust that a person will hold their calm and avoid lashing back at others?

In one of my college classes, a student surprised me by saying that he has a real problem with his own anger. This was off-topic but I could sense the appearance of a "teaching moment." A teaching moment is when the student really wants to know something and asks a question. During the class break, I took fifteen minutes and pulled together a presentation that I shared with the class. I am elaborating on the ideas here.

It helps to become a person who FLOWS with situations and does NOT succumb to a tendency to have a personal upset explode in an angry outburst. We'll use the F.L.O.W.S. process:

F - focus and express through "I-messages"
L - leave it as "I don't run that show"
O - open to assertive expressions
W - work out and rest up
S - see your fear ("Anger is fear twisted.")

1. Focus and express through "I-messages"

It's easy to feel angry if we feel like no one's listening. The truth is: the other person cannot hear you if you do not share your concerns in a non-threatening manner. When we're upset, the "non-threatening manner" is the hard part!

The answer is to express your discomfort early and use "I-messages."

Look at the difference between these two forms of communicating:

- *I-message:* "I feel frustrated when I'm kept waiting. I'm even scared when I think I may be late for work."
- *You-message:* "You're always late. You don't care if I lose my job! You only think of yourself. You're selfish!"

A problem arises if we "sit on our upset"—that is, if we do not express what bothers us until we're boiling mad.

The solution is: Prepare an I-message early and express your concern while you're still calm.

Now it's your turn.

Is there some action by another person that is bothering you?

Is it time for you to prepare an "I-message" (or two) and express your discomfort while it is still "small"?

2. Leave it as "I don't run that show"

When I say, "I don't run that show," I'm acknowledging the large amount of things that happen in the world that we do not control.

We may be able to influence certain people in certain situations. But there is much we do not control—for example, another person's feelings function on his or her time table.

A lot of anger begins when we feel that we're not going to get what we want.

One thing we do not control is if or when another person forgives us for a mistake we've made.

If you've made a mistake, and a loved one does not grant forgiveness immediately, it can feel unfair! One client said, "It's as if he forgets all the good things I've done for the last 12 years."

One of my clients Jonathan had deeply disappointed his girlfriend Sarah when he failed to pick her up on time. She had told him that on the day she heard about her parents' divorce, both parents had left her waiting at day care. She had felt abandoned. This was a traumatic event. Sarah felt that Jonathan had abandoned her.

I introduced the idea of "I don't run that show" to Jonathan. He would remain constant, doing loving actions and doing his best to make amends—this is the show that he runs.

He did not "run the show" of whether or not Sarah would or could forgive him.

Good news: She eventually forgive him. It took weeks.

The "I don't run that show" idea can save you a lot of effort. Some people (you've probably met a few) do not have much space to show compassion for others. Trying to change another person can waste your time.

Instead, we can use Jonathan's example: remain constant, do loving actions and do your best to make amends.

As for the rest, "we do not run that show."

3. Open to assertive expressions

Sometimes, we become angry when another person forcibly puts forth their opinion.

For example, Janet, one of my clients, was confronted with an angry response to one of her blog articles.

The pattern I provided for her to use in a private email to the commenter was:

Hello_____
Thank you for your comment.
It was with great sadness that I read your comment multiple times.
I agree that _____. [if you agree to a portion of their comment.]

Janet chose to respond with a private email message and she has not posted the person's original comment. (She monitors her comment section on her blog.)

Janet's email response to the "assertive" comment secured a calm reply message from the upset commenter.

My point is: "to be open to assertive expressions" is to take the viewpoint that other people CAN ask for what they want. (You do not have to say, "yes.")

Also, when I say, "Open to assertive expressions," I'm talking about making your personal comments "assertive" and NOT aggressive.

Here is the big difference:

Assertive: "I'm looking for a solution here. We can do _____ or _____."

Aggressive: "This is a horrible, [expletive] company that doesn't care about customers! I'm [expletive] angry about this poor treatment! I'm going send out an email to ____!"

Assertive comments often take preparation.

Get support. Talk with an insightful friend or a counselor and form your assertive plan before you get into a situation that might further raise your upset. It works even better when you rehearse your positive, assertive comments. We're looking to reduce the chance of an angry outburst.

Now it's your turn.

How can you form an assertive [but NOT aggressive] response to a situation that bothers you? Who can help you prepare before your next meeting with the other person?

4. Work out and rest up

A top prevention of expressing anger in a hurtful manner is to keep yourself calm and well-rested. In today's fast-paced society, that a big order!

I keep a log of my sleep. If I'm working long hours, I make adjustments and get more sleep on the next day or days.

I exercise everyday. Sometimes, I combine things like walking and talking with a friend. I make exercise a natural part of the day.

The important thing is: Keep yourself fit, strong and calm. Then you'll find that you have more patience and personal resources to face the disappointments and challenges of each day.

5. See your fear ("Anger is fear twisted.")

Over the years—in writing 22 books—I've written about my phrase "Anger is fear twisted."

Years ago, I realized that when I'm angry somewhere buried beneath it is the fear that something bad is going to happen or something I need is not going to happen.

My sweetheart has used this knowledge to ask me, "What are you afraid of?" (I suggest that you be careful about asking that question of another person. It might intensify their reaction!)

At this moment, I suggest that you ask yourself: What am I afraid of?

Then, pause and listen to your internal responses.

It really helps to write your personal answers in a journal to these questions:

- What am I afraid of?
- How might I not get what I want?
- What am I afraid that I'll lose?
- Is there another way to get what I want?
- Is there another person (other than this one) who can help me get what I want?
- What would be an assertive (NOT aggressive) way I can ask for what I want?
- How can I make sure that I am okay, even if I do not get what I want?

The above seems like a lot of work.

And, it really helps to prepare yourself and take care of

your own needs.

You will more likely stay calm and avoid an angry outburst.

And that will not only protect your relationship, it will enhance it.

Success in love, life and business is built on trust.

Can you be trusted to "hold your cool" when things get bumpy and rough?

Working on your skills for dealing with personal anger pays many dividends.

Some people say that they do not have the time to do the above preparation. Apparently, they're not paying close attention to all of the wasted time and lost opportunities that uncontrolled angry outburst create.

But this is NOT for you.

Take good care of yourself. Prepare and calmly deliver your "I-message." Discover that even if you do not always get what you want, you feel better because you have expressed your true needs. You have been courageous and proactive. And, if necessary, you can move on to other situations and other people to get what would be best for your life.

* * * * * *

Learning to personally handle your own difficult emotions is a powerful way to support your relationship. Now, Linda and Charlie Bloom pull back the curtain to reveal that "differences aren't the problem."

The Differences Aren't the Problem
by Linda and Charlie Bloom

Leah: Before Jason and I got married, I thought that couples became more harmonious over time and that their differences naturally diminished as they got to know each other better. Boy, was I wrong! Not only did our different points of view and behaviors not go away, they actually became inflamed and amplified over time. For a while it really seemed like they would be the end of our marriage.

Jason: Things looked pretty hopeless to me for quite a while. Leah and I were both caught up in this impossible cycle in which we were each trying to convert the other into seeing things our way, even though our efforts to do so were destroying the love and good will we had previously shared. I've always had a thing about being controlled and I reacted like crazy every time Leah tried to get me to do something or talk me into something that I didn't feel right about.

Leah: And that just triggered my fear that Jason didn't love me because I thought that if he did, he would be more open to my input and responsive to my concerns. My fears got me into a panic so I just amped up my efforts to influence him....

Jason: ...which not surprisingly didn't go over so well with me. We kept getting locked into these horrible reactive patterns that kept squeezing the life out of our marriage. To say that it was a nightmare would be an understatement.

Leah: We finally got some help, which we probably should have done much earlier in the process, but that was one of the issues that we couldn't agree on. I wanted to get counseling and Jason didn't.

Jason: I've always believed that if you put your mind to something and worked hard to straighten out your problems, you should be able to take care of things on your own. I got to be wrong about that! Fortunately, getting help was something that Leah took a stand on and she wouldn't back down. I knew that she meant it when she gave me the ultimatum about seeing a counselor, so I gave in and grudgingly went with her. I feel grateful to her to this day for her willingness to put our marriage on the line and take that stand. I'm convinced that we wouldn't be sitting here together today had she not done so.

Leah: For me, it didn't even feel like a risk. We literally had nothing to lose. Our relationship was completely trashed, we were living like enemies, we hadn't had sex in months, and day-to-day, things were just getting worse.

Jason: The counselor really helped us, especially me. I probably had a lot more to learn about relationships that Leah.

Leah: Fortunately Jason's a very good student. If there's something that he wants to learn about, he throws himself into it wholeheartedly, and that's the way he engaged in the counseling process. Plus, it didn't hurt that the counselor was a man who Jason could trust and relate to.

Jason: He helped me to see some of the ways that I was getting in my own way and pointed out positive alternatives to my negative behaviors. He also helped me to see that underneath my anger and desire to control Leah, was a lot of fear that Leah might see me (or I might see myself) as being weak if I didn't stand up to her. I hadn't connected the dots enough to see that I was a big part of the problem, that it wasn't just Leah that was being, at least in *my mind, stubborn and unreasonable, but that I was too.*

Leah: We both played our parts. I had to learn to understand and manage my fears of losing Jason that caused me to try to control him. One of the most important things that I learned was that it wasn't our differences that were the problem, but our efforts to convert each other to our perspective, to control each other's point of view as well as their behavior. As we each began to trust that we could have these differences, that they would not and need not go away, we both relaxed our need to get the other person on the same page as we were.

My greatest fear had been that if we didn't eliminate the differences and homogenize as a couple that our marriage would self-destruct. This fear caused me to do and say things that intensified Jason's resistance to being controlled. These days, we each just communicate our preferences and talk over things without the feeling that we need to get the other person to agree with everything that we say. Amazingly, we usually come to a workable understanding almost every single time because we never try to pressure each other into anything... well, hardly ever.

Jason: What it's taken for us to get here has been a lot of practice. Our counselor got us started but then it was up to us to practice the things that we learned from him. Changing old habits isn't easy, but fortunately for us, we had plenty of "learning opportunities". In the process we've each become more appreciative of our differences and more accepting of our respective ways of being in the world. We have both become more committed to accepting influence from each other and to stretching into the other's world.

Leah: We've also developed more tolerance, acceptance, patience, and forgiveness and we've become more skilled in the art of non-reactive listening. It's really paid off for us. For a couple of recovering "hot heads", we live a remarkably harmonious and peaceful life now. And we haven't homogenized in the process, but rather, we have become more uniquely ourselves.

Jason: We still have the same preferences and values that we had when we first met nineteen years ago, but we're learning to live with them. Leah's a cat person, I love dogs; She tends to be kind of introverted, I'm a party animal. She's very detail-focused, I look at the big picture. She likes to get to the airport three hours early, I like to get there just before they close the doors at the gate. She's very touchy-feely, me, not so much.

Leah: Jason's a night person, I'm a morning person. I'm a hopeless romantic, he's not. I'm idealistic, Jason is what he refers to as "realistic". I'm more driven by my emotions, he's more intellectually oriented. There are more differences than I could list on ten pages, but the differences are what make things interesting and help us to open our world more expansively than we would if we were with someone exactly like ourselves. But what really matters is that when it comes to the important things that we value most highly, we're both on the same page. We love each other, we value family, we both strive to live lives of integrity and honesty, we both value the learning process, and we both love to have fun!"

If the absence of irreconcilable differences were a requirement for staying married, there would be few, if any married couples alive today. Even the most successful marriages contain irreconcilable differences; those differences that cannot under any circumstances be resolved or dissolved completely. Of course, some differences can be deal-breakers if one or both partners can't tolerate the situation, but in our experience, when there is a foundation of love and respect in the relationship, this situation is less likely to occur.

Only a small portion of the differences that most couples start out with are actually solvable. The presence of differences isn't necessarily problematic. It's when they become conflictual that there is trouble. When we appreciate the value of our differences, we begin to see them not as a threat, but an enhancement to our relationship. We may even see that it was the differences themselves that initially attracted us to each other in the first place.

Leah and Jason salvaged a marriage that was on life support by being willing to make something more important than playing out life-long patterns of control and manipulation. They were willing to risk it all to go for the real gold that is available in committed partnerships. They put their relationship at the top of their priority list. There is an old saying, that "you can be right or you can have a relationship." The key word is "or". You can't have it both ways. What's your choice?

Linda and Charlie Bloom are seminar leaders, authors, psychotherapists and consultants and are considered experts in the field of human relations. They have been working with individuals, couples, and groups throughout the country and internationally since 1975 and have been featured speakers at many professional and public conferences. They have made over 200 radio and TV appearances.

They have been faculty members and educators at a number of learning institutes and universities including Esalen Institute, The Kripalu Center, The Crossings, JFK University, Omega Institute, California Institute of Integral Studies, California School of Professional Psychology,

Antioch University, the Institute for Transpersonal Psychology, and many others. Their work has been endorsed by Marianne Williamson, Gay and Kathlyn Hendricks, Dr. Laura Schlessinger, Jerry Jampolsky, Stephen Levine, and many other nationally recognized speakers and educators.

Linda and Charlie have been married since 1972 and have three grandchildren. Together they co-direct Bloomwork in Santa Cruz, CA. For more information please visit their website: www.Bloomwork.com.

Website: bloomwork.com

Books: They are the authors of *101 Things I Wish I Knew When I Got Married: Simple Lessons to Make Love Last*, published in 2004 which has sold over 100,000 copies. Their latest book, *Secrets of a Great Marriages: Real Truth from Real Couples about Lasting Love* was published 2010.

Contact Information: Office: 831-421-9822, or by email at: lcbloom@bloomwork.com.

* * *

Now, I'll share Dr. Elayne Savage's insights on supporting your relationships.

How To De-Clutter Your Relationships
by Elayne Savage, PhD

Misunderstandings damage work and personal relationships. Feelings get hurt. Someone feels rejected. Sometimes anger takes over. Before you know it, resentment creeps into every nook and cranny of your relationship. Isn't it time to clear it out and make room for respect and connection and enhanced communication?

Relationships can benefit from a good "spring cleaning."

It gets rid of the clutter.

Why not toss out things you've been stockpiling? You could chuck misunderstandings. Hurl your hurt feelings. Toss out anger and resentments.

Even small misunderstandings can lead to hurt feelings. Someone says or does something (or neglects to say or do it.) The other person takes it personally. Feelings get hurt. Anger takes over. Before you know it, resentment begins to creep into every nook and cranny.

And your relationship gets de-railed.

Stockpiling All Those Hurts

This is exactly what happened between Allison and Terry. Allison found herself getting upset whenever Terry came home later than agreed upon.

Allison would begin to worry and the anxiety would build. By the time Terry walked through the door, she blasted all of her pent up fury. She began to recite a litany of all the times this has happened in the past.

Even when Terry made an effort to call her if he was running late, Allison acted hurt that he disregarded their agreement.

Finally she gathered the courage to talk with Terry directly and honestly. She told him how hurt and disrespected she felt each time he arrived later than their agreed upon time. She asked him not to be so quick to agree to a time that was really not realistic.

Once she was able to put words to her feelings Allison could begin to clear out her built up resentment. She discovered space was opening up.

Enough space where she and Terry could bring positive feelings, respect and energy back into their relationship.

Clearing Out Resentments

Think for a moment about how much space resentment takes up. Sometimes there is barely room for connection or intimacy.

Clearing out resentments creates the space we need to renew respect and get back on track.

This goes for work relationships too. The roadblocks to successful relationships are the same: Feeling rejected or the fear of rejection. Feeling misunderstood, disappointed and not appreciated.

A key to productive relationships is mutual respect. Sure, we all have style differences. However we don't have to let this lead to relationship problems.

Instead of feeling threatened by your differences, why not create space to honor them? Why not make an effort to respect others even though they may think or act differently than you do?

Feeling accepted and respected is vital to productive work and personal relationships. But what if you don't feel this acceptance coming from the other person? Non-acceptance feels like disrespect. In other words we tend to translate feeling "dissed" into feeling rejected.

It's especially painful to feel dismissed or discounted or dispensable. Rejection hurts. We tend to collect these kinds of hurts. We pile it into containers. We store it up in the form of resentments.

When we feel hurt trust begins to erode and resentment grows in its place. Resentment turns into anger and anger mutates into alienation. You begin to realize that these negative feelings are beginning to take up so much space in your relationship that there's barely room for connection (or intimacy.)

Misreadings and Miscues

The source of the most relationship problems is fuzzy communication. Unclear communication leads to misunderstandings which can lead to disappointments. And all too often disappointments feel like rejection.

You may think you're giving a clear message, but, in fact, the only thing you are giving out are hints or indirect requests. Do you find yourself getting upset because your partner or coworker misreads you. After all, if they care about you, they'll read your mind! Right?

All too often we give out confusing mixed messages. For example, Janie asks Jordan, "Could you pick up a color cartridge for me at the office supply store, if you get the chance?" Jordan takes her "if you get the chance" to mean it's no big deal if he does or doesn't. Janie is upset when he doesn't show up with the cartridge, thinking he's dismissing her request. She takes it personally, thinking, "If he cares about me, he'd do this favor for me—I must not be important to him." Janie feels rejected and resentful. She doesn't realize how she dismissed her own request as not really important.

How do we keep from getting hurt when disappointments seem to be lurking around every corner?

Seven Surefire Ways to Avoid Disappointment in Relationships

- Try not to have unrealistic expectations/anticipations
- Don't put someone on a pedestal or make them your icon
- Don't get involved with "potential," hoping to change them

- Don't look for "proof" of love—hoping the person will read your mind
- Try not to fool yourself into believing exaggerated promises
- Avoid having hidden agendas and secret contracts
- Be sure and check things out with the other person

Is It Really OK to Ask for What You Need?

Another way of avoiding disappointments is by recognizing what you do need and asking for it. The trouble is as children many of us became expert at anticipating the needs of others—we never gave ourselves permission to have needs. As adults, we have to practice recognizing that we have needs and it's OK!

Practice asking yourself:

- "What would make me feel good today?" "What do I want?" "What do I need?"
- "From whom?" (Yourself? Someone else?)
- "In what way? What form would it take?"
- And then ask yourself "how I would know this need is met?"

Our relationships would go more smoothly if we could clearly communicate what matters to us. When we expect our partner or friends or coworkers to read between the lines, it's just a set-up for hurt feelings, anger and resentment. Why not think about it as a "space" issue. Would you rather fill up space with resentment? Or do you opt for connection and intimacy in your relationships?

Getting Back on the Respect Track

So how can you get your relationship back on the respect track?

Here's a tip that works for both personal and professional relationships: Rather than continuing to be put off by your partner's or co-worker's "ways", try to find something you really respect about them. Granted this may be a whole lot harder with someone at work.

Do you appreciate their smile, intelligence or sense of humor? What about their taste in clothes or colors? Once you can do that, try to focus in on this characteristic while you are talking with them.

When they see respect in your eyes they just might respond in kind. You'll be amazed at how quickly the situation can change for the better.

You may even notice some respect coming right back at you!

Elayne Savage, PhD, is a professional speaker, workplace coach, psychotherapist, and the author of *Breathing Room— Creating Space To Be a Couple* and *Don't Take It Personally! The Art of Dealing with Rejection*. She lives in Berkeley, CA and can be contacted through her website

www.queenofrejection.com

For more communication tips:

Blog: 'Tips from The Queen of Rejection'®

Twitter@ElayneSavage

LinkedIn.com/in/elaynesavage

* * * * *

Topic #4
Book Four: Enjoy Life's Many Facets

Untangle Yourself from the Ego-self and Then Support Your Relationship

Your Ego-self is that part of you which feels small and vulnerable. So in a relationship, your Ego-self says, "Everything *you* do hurts me." You can imagine how much trouble that creates for your relationship.

When the Ego-self is running the show, romance goes out the window. Why? Your partner now feels under attack and his or her energy that would go to having positive feelings is unfortunately trapped in trying to defend the self.

Often, when people say, "I've got to protect myself," they're referring to protecting the Ego-self.

You see you actually have three selves.

Ego Self – that part of you that feels vulnerable and small. (In other words, the ego is made of fear.)

Observer Self – that part of you that calmly views what is going on.

True Self – that part of you that feels connected to other people and to the universe as a whole.

Being stuck in the Ego-self is natural. Why? It actually relates to parts of the human brain. The emotional brain (made of the brain stem and amygdala) is focused on protecting you from loss. The reptile brain (made of the brain stem) is focused solely on survival.

Any sight or sound immediately gets the emotional

brain's and reptile brain's attention. Researchers note that any painful experience is immediately turned into a long-term memory. That is, the emotional brain and reptile brain facilitate the long-term memory of pain.

On the other hand, it takes 10 to 20 seconds of focused attention to get a positive experience into your long-term memory.

What this means is: you and I need to become skillful so that we can unleash ourselves from the clutches of the frightened Ego-self.

I refer to something I call the *Tyranny of the Ego*, which relates to how the ego keeps us frightened . . . and a frightened mind has fewer resources. A frightened mind centers on thoughts like:

- Will I get hurt?
- How can I play in a way to avoid losing? [That's the opposite of the proactive stance of aiming to win.]

To free yourself of limits is to practice ways of releasing yourself from the ego.

Between stimulus and response there is a space. In that space is our power to choose our response. In our response lies our growth and our freedom. – Viktor E. Frankl

How to Free Yourself of the Limits of the Ego-self

Step One:
One primary way to free yourself of the distractions of the Ego-self is to pause and do deep breathing. Calm yourself down.

Try it now. Breathe in through your nose (if possible) and have your belly expand. Hold your breath for a moment.

Then breathe out through your mouth and have your belly deflate. Repeat three times. (This is called belly breathing.)

Step Two:
View the situation from the Observer Self. One method is to view your thoughts as leaves that flow past on a river. Do not obsess on one thought. Let it flow onward with the other thoughts.

Step Three:
Use this phrase to focus your thoughts: *Different but good.* (The idea is to find something good or at least neutral in what is occurring. The truth is: no matter how well we plan, things often turn out differently than our first imagining. Here is another phrase you can use: *It is what it is.*)

Step Four:
Now, from the calmness of the Observer Self, consider how you might respond to the given situation. See how you might have a kind, human connection to whoever is involved in the situation.

For example, I have an elderly relative who actually destroyed my gift to her, right before my eyes. It was a malicious move on her part.

My Ego-self had a fleeting thought: "I'll buy her a book next time, and I'll rip it apart in front of her." Then, I took a breath and let my upset thought go by (like on a river). My Observer Self held to the idea: "I do not return negativity for negativity."

So now, I'm free to act from my kind, compassionate True Self. Remember your True Self is that part of you that feels connected to other people and the universe.

With compassion, I see that my distraught elderly relative is a human being who did not learn how to deal with upset feelings. For decades, I have heard her say, "You make me mad" to various family members. She has no intention to learn things. So I just reduce my exposure to her.

Now it's your turn.

Are you facing something that gives you an immediate feeling of having to protect yourself?

Realize that using belly breathing and your Observer Self helps you think more clearly. Of course, sometimes, we actually must protect ourselves and do what's necessary.

Other times, we just feel that our ego was bruised, and it helps to get ourselves to calmness and the Observer Self.

From there you can take the next step; you can experience the compassion, connection and peace of your True Self.

Practice the process of freeing yourself from your Ego-self. Then you'll have the energy to support your relationship, and you'll feel better.

* * * * * *

Topic #5
Book Four: Enjoy Life's Many Facets

How You Can Make the Crucial Difference (The Power of Listening)

The bullet stopped two hearts. Then the widow's heart continued beating. My neighbor is crying now. Why? Today (12-11-13) her husband was shot dead at his workplace.

Have you ever been called to try to comfort someone during a tragedy?

Here are three vital things to do that I've learned through

tough experience and from mentors.

1. It's not about what you say; it's about your listening to what they say.

I've noticed that some people fret about what they might say to be of comfort to someone who is deeply grieving.

Instead, let's drop the focus on what we say, and devote ourselves to making a safe space for the other person to express her feelings. All of them.

What to say? Sometimes, a simple: "I'm here. I'm listening" is just what is needed.

2. Do *not* disappear.

A close friend told me that when her mother died, a number of her friends simply disappeared. Perhaps, they were confused about what to do. Or maybe they could not face the pain one feels when they can't change anything.

I invite you to avoid "disappearing." Do what you can. Attend the funeral and give a hug to the one grieving. Make an appearance. You do not need to stay a long time. Just make sure to be there for the grieving person for some of the time.

[On 12-15-13, I attended the funeral. I stood up and went to the podium and said, "I was [his name]'s neighbor. He was kind and helped my sweetheart and me — with tech/computer problems, of course. I only need to say — Thank you [his name] for your kindness." I choked up when saying that final sentence, and I sat down. I include this brief example because it demonstrates making an appearance. His mother came up to me and said, "Thanks for speaking up."]

3. Make sure *you* take breaks and renew your energy.

I know from experience that a lot of crying creates a bad

headache. In order to support another person, you must also support yourself. Take shifts with other people as you, as a team, support the grieving person. When someone else takes a shift and stays with the grieving person, do something for yourself. Take a nap. See a movie and get your mind off the grieving—for a time.

In order to be strong for someone else, you need energy. Be a hero: recharge yourself and then return to support the grieving person.

The truth is: some of the most intense and toughest moments that require courage are actually quiet moments. Listening is one of the toughest things we can do. When you listen well, you restrain yourself from offering your opinions. When I am with a grieving person, I find that I cry, too. So being there requires me to confront pain, too.

Good listeners are heroes.

When people grieve, it is an important time for us to stretch and extend compassion.

Get rest. Be strong. And then step in and provide your listening and support.

You'll be proud yourself.

You'll provide the kindness this world needs.

* * *

Above, I mentioned that *good listeners are heroes*. It takes a lot of personal energy and skill to be a good listener. This means a lot to me because I have a couple of elderly family members who have never applied themselves to listening well. And I've seen the emotional destruction that occurs when someone basically insults another person by refusing to listen.

Here are my thoughts on listening well:

Do you want to get people to like you and trust you quickly? Learn to listen well. Here are three methods:

A – attend
R – reflect
E – engage emotions

1. Attend

Give your full attention. Make sure that your heart faces their heart ("Heart faces heart.")

At times, I begin a conversation with, "I'm listening. What would you like me to know about the situation?" The reason for this beginning is sometimes the situation may have some heat to it. When I listen first, the tension drains from the situation.

Think about it: How often does one get fully listened to? Can you imagine what a relief it is to have your thoughts and feelings heard without interruption or automatic judgment?

Near the end of a conversation, I ask, "Is there anything else you need me to know?" Again, this is about giving full attention.

2. Reflect

Provide what I call "Reflective Replies." Reflect their concerns and emotions. Say things like: "That sounds frustrating" or "That sounds hard to endure."

Why is this valuable?

First, we often do not know if someone understands the meaning behind our words. Reflective Replies assure the speaker that you understand the meaning. Or if you say something a bit off, the speaker can use other words to clarify his or her meaning.

Second, you do NOT tell another person what he or she is feeling. You provide a gentle phrase: "That sounds . . ."

For example, you might say, "That sounds frustrating." But the person says, "Not frustrating, disappointing."

You can ask, "What disappointed you the most about this situation?" That question signals that you are being fully present with the person in the moment.

3. Engage emotions

Help the person feel it is safe to share his or her feelings. Someone may say, "That driver made me mad." Often, I'll reply, "Okay." For me "okay" is neutral. I do not have to agree. By saying "okay" I'm communicating, "I'm hearing you. It's okay to feel whatever you're feeling."

I have an elderly relative who has horrible habits when it comes to listening. This guy only pauses for a breath between things he wants to say. It does NOT feel safe to express a feeling around him. I have actually said, "You cannot logic me out of my feelings. I get to feel the way I feel about this."

Instead, as a good listener, you make a safe place for the other person to express his or her feelings. Once a person feels heard, often the energy about a situation "cools off."

Listening well is a big part of creating success and fulfillment in our lives.

How do you get loyalty and reliable efforts from other people? Listen to them well.

Start practicing today.

You'll discover how your business and personal relationships improve.

* * *

Listening is so important, I'm now sharing Craig Harrison's thoughts on this vital topic.

Listen Up!
Hone Your Listening Skills for Success
by Craig Harrison

So much attention is focused on what to say and how to say it.

In speeches, debates and conversation, we are obsessed with our message and how to express ourselves. Sometimes, this focus obscures our listening.

Listening skills are key to our success as communicators, leaders, servers and as human beings.

Any discussion on the importance of listening—vis-à-vis speaking—should acknowledge the fact that we were born with two ears and just one mouth. The implication: we should listen twice as much as we speak!

Believe it or not, Listening is a learned skill. While we are blessed with ears to hear with, listening is more than just hearing. *Listening* involves an active engagement.

By definition Listening means:
"applying oneself to hearing something"

DID YOU KNOW...?
Here are some facts about listening, courtesy of colleague Louisa Rogers, Louisa Rogers Communications, in Eureka, CA (www.LouisaRogers.com):

1. All communication is received ... but 70-90% of the data is screened out or altered by the receiver. So what you say is

NOT necessarily what the listener gets.

2. Listening is (incorrectly) not perceived as powerful by most people.

3. We have a strong cultural tendency to tune out. Our minds go forward (What do I say next? How do I defend myself? What shall I have for lunch?), or in reverse (Did I turn the car lights off? Did I get an e-mail back from...?).

4. Rates of speaking / listening: We listen at 1,000-1,200 words a minute. We speak at 300 words a minute. Thus, our minds wander.

Based on Louisa's findings I believe the following: where there's a will, there are ways to become a better listener.

DON'T JUST DO SOMETHING...LISTEN!

Alas, we can become better listeners once we set our mind and ears to it.

Vow to become a better listener.

1. Monitor your own listening: where do you follow the speaker and where do you tune out? Analyze for yourself why it is you tune out where you do.

2. Suspend judgment when you listen, focusing instead on comprehension. Many times we immerse ourselves in our own analysis of what is heard: do I agree or disagree? Focus instead on comprehension.

3. Listen for the meta-message: the message within the message. Sometimes what people AREN'T saying is also insightful. Listen between the lines.

4. Become an Active Listener: listen with your ears, mind,

head and heart. Concentrate on listening as if you will be tested on what this person has said and need to share it with a class of strangers. Can you do it?

5. Active listening involves not only following along with the speaker, but letting him or her know you are tracking their message. Use nods, gestures and utterances to convey comprehension or confusion, so they receive feedback you are with them, or not. A furrowed brow, a tilt of the head or squinting signals to them you are confused. A nod, a smile or other gestures indicates understanding.

6. Remember that confirming understanding doesn't imply concordance. Confirming your comprehension of one's communication doesn't automatically mean you agree with everything.

7. Short phrases are useful to your listener. Saying:
"I see"
"yep"
"uh-huh!"
"hmmm"
conveys understanding.
Phrases like:
"huh?"
"I'm not sure I understand"
"what do you mean?"
"please elucidate"
let the listener know you are hazy about their meaning.

8. A great way to confirm for your listener and yourself that you understand is to periodically paraphrase or replay what you believe you heard. It's a reality check that allows

you both to continue with confidence.

Whether you are brokering peace in the Middle East or a squabble with a family member at the dinner table, I find wisdom in Stephen Covey's proscription to "seek first to understand, then to be understood."

So hang out your "Hear Here" sign, follow this sound advice and listen for success!

Craig Harrison's Expressions of Excellence!™ helps organizations express their sales and service excellence and its professionals become better communicators and leaders. His presentations, books, courses and coaching empower adults worldwide to shape their world. Based in the San Francisco Bay Area Craig travels the world as chief expressionist to foster excellence for you! For more information visit www.ExpressionsOfExcellence.com or call (510) 547-0664.

* * * * * *

Topic #6
Book Four: Enjoy Life's Many Facets
Soulful Time Management

Soulful Time Management is a process of manifesting more inner peace during our daily lives. An old phrase emphasizes: "Be in the world, not of it."

A major focus of Soulful Time Management is realizing that the true source of our inner peace is spirit-related. In this section, we explore *10 Primary Areas*. Using the methods of Soulful Time Management helps us *save time* in that we avoid the chaos caused by ego-centered living. Focusing on soul-focused methods helps us reduce mental clutter.

It helps a lot when you can make a shift from feeling stressed out to calming down. This became clear to me several years ago. It was night time in San Francisco. My then sweetheart and I were walking down the sidewalk when I heard a noise behind us. I glanced back as a bicycle with riders careened toward us! Acting quickly, I pushed my sweetheart out of the way. I pivoted, and the bike's handlebar struck my coattail. The bike sped off with two riders, one riding on the handlebars (no wonder the driver couldn't see).

Immediately, I assured myself that my sweetheart was okay. Luckily she was fine, but her face showed fear and irritation. I was upset and felt my anger rising as I realized that she could have been hurt. The thoughtless act could have ended in serious injury, and my anger flashed as I focused on that. My thoughts flowed rapidly through this process:

1) "They could have hurt my sweetheart."
2) "But no one was hurt."
3) "They're just kids."
4) "Can I teach them anything by shouting after them?"

The answer was No. This was not a *teaching moment*, when another person is read or interested in learning. So I repeated a SwitchPhrase (for switching the direction of my thoughts)—"Let it go." Within seconds, I breathed easier and felt better. I could turn my thoughts and energy to enjoying the evening with my sweetheart.

Spiritual principles mentioned in this section are emphasized by many spiritual traditions.

Experience Happiness

Happiness cannot be traveled to, owned, earned, worn or

consumed. Happiness is the spiritual experience of living every minute with love, grace, and gratitude. – Denis Waitley

Happiness is not something ready made. It comes from your own actions. – The Dalai Lama

Our task is to expand our perceptions so that we can experience happiness on a day-to-day and moment-to-moment basis.

Method #1: Focus on Gratitude
Barry Neil Kaufman, the author of *Happiness is A Choice*, emphasizes that happiness includes being in the state of gratitude. I invite my clients to consider the process I call *The 10 Blessings.* You can switch the direction of your thoughts by making a mental checklist of ten parts of your life for which you're grateful. By expressing thoughts like "I'm grateful for my friends: Dave, Stephanie, James" and "I'm grateful for the prosperity from my job," we turn our thoughts and feelings to a happier state.

Feeling Renewed
Not what we have, but what we enjoy, constitutes our abundance. – Epicurus

Higher Power's abundance is everywhere. It is up to us to push aside our perceptions of scarcity and lack. Releasing judgments is a crucial part of this process.

Method #2: Re-create, Renew, Release Judgments
To feel renewed, we need to let go of judgment which weighs us down. Each judgment is like a marble that we swallow. It is no wonder that by the end of the day we feel

weighed down and tired (thanks to author Roger Mellot for his analogy).

I know a new business owner who expressed this judgment: "One year has gone by, and I have nothing to show for it." This judgment does *not* energize the business owner.

I suggested that she consider some empowering thoughts: "Everything that I have done has planted seeds. Higher power will show me which seeds will blossom. I trust that Higher Power will guide me to refine my approach to business. And if I need to change something, Higher Power will guide me."

My name for this process of replacing thoughts is using *SwitchPhrases*. Now, the business owner has a phrase, "Everything I am doing is planting seeds." The SwitchPhrase becomes a reflexive response when depressing thoughts rise up like weeds.

Experiencing Inner Peace

Your ego focuses on holding grievances. Your ego maintains if some external circumstance were changed, you would feel saved.
– A Course In Miracles

Inner peace is accessible on a moment-to-moment basis. We need to develop the perception that our inner peace is separate from external events.

Method #3: Devote time to breathing and meditation

One way to experience inner peace, regardless of external events, is through breathing and meditation. Here is simple of version of this process. You can breathe in through your nose and recite (in your mind) an affirmation (such as "Higher Power relaxes me.") Then hold your breath while you recite your affirmation again. Then breathe out while internally reciting your affirmation once more. Breathing in this way ten times is what I call *Affirm-breathing*. As a simple version of meditating, you can close your eyes and repeat your affirmation over and over. Or you just observe your breathing. At some point, you'll lose track of time and your words. Great! It's that experience of no thought and no time that gives us a taste of the infinite and inner peace. You can breathe and mediate for as little as six to fifteen minutes (perhaps, upon awakening, or during lunch time in your parked car, or at night just before falling asleep).

Feed Your Spirit
Out beyond ideas of wrongdoing and rightdoing, there is a field. I will meet you there. – Rumi

Where there is no vision, the people perish. – Proverbs 29:18

Method #4: Feed your spirit.
Have you noticed how some people get all caught up in trying to convince others that they alone are "right." I've learned that feeding my mind and spirit with nutritional books and audio programs like sacred texts and positive, motivation audio programs helps me move beyond an ego-focused obsession with "proving I'm right."

For example, I find it uplifting to listen to a spiritual text on audio. Uplifting books and audio programs are sources for ideas of faith, belief and vision. Many people limit their exposure to the news before going to bed and instead focus that time on activities that feed their spirit.

Connection with Other People
Thousands of candles can be lighted from a single candle, and the life of the candle will not be shortened. Happiness never

decreases by being shared. – The Buddha

A number of spiritual texts emphasize that we already have a connection with others and with Higher Power. We just need to shift our perceptions to our true connection.

Method #5: Use Closeness Rituals

A *Closeness Ritual* is something that we do that provides the opportunity for developing more closeness with someone important to us. Here are examples: a Saturday one-on-one lunch with your child, a monthly house meeting among roommates sharing an apartment, an after-work cup of coffee with a co-workers, or a weekly date-night with your romantic partner.

Turning from the Ego to Higher Power's Love

I look upon the ego as nothing more than an idea that each of us has about ourselves. The ego is only an illusion, but a very influential one. Letting the ego-illusion become your identity can prevent you from knowing your true self. – Dr. Wayne Dyer

We have the power to experience inner peace and happiness. It is by turning away from ego-related perceptions that we begin to feel the joy and love that Higher Power provides. Ego-related perceptions are fear-based, and we feel better when we focus on love.

Method #6: Focus your language on solutions

We turn away from ego-related perceptions and fears by focusing our language on solutions. A powerful way to focus on solutions is to carefully select our own stories that we tell others. Roger Mellot, author of *Stress Management for Professionals*, explained that he used to tell the story of how his older brother died while Roger was a young boy. An insightful woman asked Roger, "Why did you tell that story?" Roger realized that he had been looking for sympathy. In the years following that conversation, Roger turned his focus to telling stories that uplift other people and his own spirit.

Nurturing Yourself
The secret of health for both mind and body is not to mourn for the past, not to worry about the future...but to live the present moment wisely and earnestly. – The Buddha

Nurturing yourself is a divine calling. Why? When you nurture yourself, you increase your capacity to do that which is kind and loving.

Method #7: Listen to your emotional self
We can nurture ourselves by first listening to our emotional self, sometimes referred to as the inner child. Here is an easy process. On a piece of paper, draw a line down the center. On the left side write "Inner Parent" and on the right side write "Inner Child." Now for about fifteen minutes engage in a *Dialogue with Emotional Self on Paper*. Write questions on the inner parent side: "Inner child, how are you feeling? What do you want? How can I help you feel better? What is missing right now? What would you like to happen?" Write down your immediate answers on the right side. Some thoughts might include: "I want to see that new movie about toys" and "I want to go Disneyland." If you have any evaluating thoughts (like "that's silly") write those on the inner parent side. One time, while conducting a seminar and describing this process, I suddenly felt like seeing a whimsical movie. The next day I saw the silly movie as a response to my emotional self. I felt great! Taking care of

my emotional self released a burst of energy that I applied to my work as a speaker-author. When your emotional self knows that its needs will be taken care of, you discover that you have more energy for joy and healing.

Nurturing your vehicle — your body
Use the body to bring spiritual wholeness and the body becomes holy. – A Course in Miracles

Spiritual texts show us that there are holy uses for the body. Our body is our vehicle through the journey of life. Some of us take excellent care of our car, and the well-maintained car *supports* our activities. Doesn't it make sense to do the same for our bodies?

Method #8: Exercise
I've written about "Be Happy and Fit while You're Busy." Here are two keys: 1) use an easy system and 2) make it convenient. It helps to connect things in your daily routine. For example, if you watch television and ride a stationary bicycle at the same time — that's part of an "easy system." During the week, you can log how you exercise each day. Keep a log that shows something like:
- Monday: Walked during lunch time
- Tuesday: 15 minute of aerobics while watching an exercise video DVD.
- Wednesday: Jogged six blocks
- Thursday: Met a friend and had a walking get-together.

For your spirit and for feeling good, consider the convenience of listening to spiritual texts on audio while you ride a stationary bicycle.

Finding Your Contribution or Purpose

Although the world is full of suffering, it is also full of the overcoming of it. – Helen Keller

I don't know what your destiny will be, but one thing I know: the only ones among you who will be really happy are those who will have sought and found how to serve.
– Albert Schweitzer

Various spiritual texts emphasize that happiness is related to making a contribution to other people's lives. For example, a person serving customers in a restaurant can "save the world" with kind words and friendly service—and brighten the customers' day.

Method #9: Find your contribution/purpose

Here is one of my favorite examples of bringing Higher Power into the process of finding your contribution or purpose. One of my friends searched for a name for her business. She asked Higher Power for a name but felt she wasn't receiving guidance. Then she changed her question to "How may I serve the world?" The name for her business flashed into her mind.

Free Up Time and Energy through Forgiveness

Holding on to anger, resentment and hurt only gives you tense muscles, a headache and a sore jaw from clenching your teeth. Forgiveness gives you back the laughter and the lightness in your life. – Joan Lunden

Forgiveness is ending the cycle of blame and suffering.
– Dr. Fred Luskin

Method #10: Use Forgiveness to free up time and energy

An old phrase says, "Forgiveness is for giving." What do we give? We give tolerance; we give understanding. We give a second chance. We give ourselves the grander view that we are spirits and that a person's hurtful remark cannot touch our true essence as a spirit. Recently, I have seen opportunities for forgiveness in how people send email messages to each other. I have noticed that sometimes people will send a reply email that will refute, point-by-point, the ideas of another person. Instead, a forgiving response is to avoid sending a defensive email message that would further escalate the matter by refuting the refutations point-by-point.

A better action would be to respond with a gentle comment: "Thank you for giving me information."

We can also respond, "I'd prefer to discuss this with you. How about we get together for 5 or 10 minutes . . . or have a phone conversation? In such a discussion, we can listen to the other person first, then ask, "Is there anything else?" After a time of listening, then we might add a few of our ideas to the conversation.

Conclusion:

Here is a list of the *10 Methods of Soulful Time Management.* **(By doing these activities, we save time. That is,** *we avoid the time lost* **to chaos created by one's ego.)**

#1: Focus on Gratitude
#2: Re-create, Renew, Release Judgments
#3: Devote Time to Breathing and Meditation
#4: Feed Your Spirit
#5: Use Closeness Rituals

#6: Focus Your Language on Solutions
#7: Listen to Your Emotional Self
#8: Exercise
#9: Find your Contribution/Purpose
#10: Use Forgiveness to Free Up Time and Energy

When we take action to develop clarity on how we can expand our service, we discover more joy and energy.

To add to this discussion, I'll now share **7 Principles of Soulful Time Management**

Here's the S.O.U.L.F.U.L. process:

S - Start something good today.

Do something of value today—even for 15 minutes. Write a paragraph of a book. Call a friend and ask, "How can I be supportive of what you're doing?"

O - Open your heart to good feelings and record good news

Note anything that goes well today in your *Daily Journal of Victories and Blessings*. Entries can be: exercised 20 minutes, read an uplifting book for 10 minutes, or called a friend.

U - Uncover space for Higher Power to step in.

Author Robert H. Schuller emphasized that we need to have dreams big enough so that we need God's help to fulfill them. One way to create space is to ask for guidance as you have a meditation period. You can ask for Higher Power's help by closing your eyes before you write a report (for example). Sometimes, it helps to ask for Higher Power's help, then open a book at random and see what you find. The few words might spark an idea in your mind that you can use like a springboard.

L - Life someone up a bit.

Nurture someone you meet by giving the person a smile or a compliment. Help a co-worker by passing on a useful tip or method.

F - Focus on inner peace.

Devote 6 to 15 minutes to breathing and meditating. Go "to the silence" and let Higher Power and inner peace fill you.

U - Uplift and nurture yourself.

Do something today that nurtures you. Take a bath, listen to relaxing music, see an uplifting video.

L - Link empowering feelings to the task.

If you find yourself procrastinating on a task, use one or more of these methods: 1) link a reward to the task, 2) use a method to transform the task into something more pleasant (perhaps, listen to music), and 3) note how the task will bring you closer to living a dream—and how you feel good when enjoying a new facet of life.

Remember to devote time to nurture your soul.

* * *

Since we've discussed time management, I want to be specific about *saving time* as you seek to increase your prosperity. Along that line, I'll now share C.J. Hayden's insights:

Get More Clients By Doing Less
by C.J. Hayden

I've been hearing from a lot of tired entrepreneurs lately. "I'm tired of going to networking events," they say, or, "I'm tired of always having to think up new stuff to post online." They're working pretty hard at marketing, it seems—networking, blogging, posting to social media, speaking, making calls, sending out e-mail blasts, and more.

When they don't get the results they want from marketing, entrepreneurs usually try to take on more. If their focus has been on in-person marketing, they begin marketing online. Or if they have been writing articles and blogging and being active on social media, they decide to start speaking and giving workshops. Or if they've been going to lots of events and lunches and coffee dates, they add in a call-mail-call campaign.

Huff, puff... It makes me tired just to write about all that activity.

What if the answer was actually to be found in the opposite direction? What if instead of doing more to get clients, you should really be doing less?

Here's an example of what I mean. A client I'll call Rhoda was trying to build her psychotherapy practice with a dozen different marketing approaches. She was going to professional meetings, posting flyers around her neighborhood, advertising in several directories, maintaining a Facebook page, trying to optimize her website, and more. She was tired, overwhelmed, and still didn't have enough clients.

I asked Rhoda where her best clients had come from so far—those who paid her full fee and continued to work with her over time. It turns out they had all been referrals from other professionals. I suggested that Rhoda stop everything she was currently doing about marketing, and concentrate on referral building. She was to identify a few categories of professionals who were likely to refer clients in her market niche, and get to know some people in those professions better.

When I checked in with Rhoda a few weeks later, she had already gotten some referrals from new people she had gotten to know. It was clear that if she kept working on building referral relationships with appropriate professionals, more clients would result. "Why didn't I ever do this before?" Rhoda said. "This is so much easier than all that other stuff I was doing, and it obviously works better."

Another client—I'll call him Doug—was seeking more small business clients for his IT consulting business. He was writing a blog and spending a lot of time on several social media platforms. When we first spoke, he was trying to decide whether he should launch a podcast, offer a webinar series, or both.

"What's your follow-up strategy?" I asked Doug. He wasn't sure. I tried again: "Okay, how many prospects do you have in your pipeline?" He didn't know that either. In fact, a bit more probing determined that Doug didn't have a pipeline, or a follow-up strategy. He was simply trying to be more visible online, and hoping that as a result, clients who needed him would contact him.

My suggestion to Doug was that before he spent any more effort on becoming visible, he should put in place a strategy for identifying, capturing, and following up with likely prospects.

Doug decided to offer a free phone consultation to business owners who met a few qualifying criteria. He posted about his offer in his blog and on social media. One of his first free consultations turned into a new client, and two other consultations generated clients later on when Doug followed up with them. Doug never did launch a podcast or webinar series; he didn't need them.

A woman I'll call Mara was a student in one of my classes. She had diligently been attending several new networking events per week, and was regularly meeting many people. She asked me how she could find new places to network, because only a handful of the people she met had become clients so far. And maybe they could be breakfast meetings, because her calendar was already so full at lunch and in the evenings.

Mara was surprised—and relieved—when I suggested that finding even more places to network might not be the best approach. "What if you were to choose just a handful of those networking groups," I proposed, "go back to the same ones on a regular basis, and become better acquainted with the other members?" Mara agreed to try this out, focusing on those groups where she had found the highest concentration of people in her market niche.

I ran into Mara again at a speaking engagement some months later. "You were so right about networking," she told me. "When I stopped running around to all those different places, and became a regular, people started to recognize me, and then they started to do business with me."

Are you tired of doing so much marketing? Maybe it's time to discover how you could do less. Ask yourself, like Rhoda, what is the one thing you've done to market yourself so far that had the biggest impact. Could you do more of that? Or, like Doug, determine how you can take better advantage of the visibility you already have. Or, like Mara, stop for a moment and wonder if there is a more effective way to employ the tactics you're already using.

Entrepreneurs do tend to work hard. But I'll bet you'd much rather work hard at your profession, and get paid for it, than to spend all your entrepreneurial energy getting clients in the first place.

C.J. Hayden, MCC, CPCC, is the bestselling author of *Get Clients Now!, The One-Person Marketing Plan Workbook,* and over 400 articles. C.J. is a business coach and teacher who helps entrepreneurs get clients, get strategic, and get things done. Her company, Wings for Business, specializes in serving self-employed professionals and solopreneurs.

A popular speaker and workshop leader, C.J. has presented hundreds of programs on marketing and entrepreneurship to corporate clients, professional associations, and small businesses. She has taught marketing for John F. Kennedy University, Mills College, the U.S. Small Business Administration, and SCORE. She contributes regularly to dozens of magazines and websites, including *Home Business, RainToday, Salesopedia,* and About.com.

WEBSITE: www.getclientsnow.com
CONTACT: info@getclientsnow.com (877) 946-4722

* * * * *

Topic #6
Book Four: Enjoy Life's Many Facets
Replace Fear with Love

One year when I was working for a major corporation, I was leaving for the evening. A co-worker who had chosen to work overtime, said, "Some of us have endurance." His tone of voice implied, "I'm better than you." I had a momentary feeling of irritation. I also felt fear based on the thought, "If this person doesn't like me, he might make me look bad to my boss." But I remembered that I could chose to be in *love-mode*, and I responded, "I appreciate that you're working hard." With that, I left to enjoy my evening. I felt light because I did *not* participate in the negative feelings. Also, I acknowledged his efforts with appreciation.

Love is feeling one's spirit, and responding to events in a positive manner. Truly, our spirit is bigger than just our temporary feelings of hurt.

Staying in what I call *love-mode* is a process of creating peace in your life. The process of forgiveness is part of this approach to your world. Some individuals find it difficult to accept the concept of forgiveness when they see injustice in the world. When children are hurt, many of us feel our peace of mind shattered. Some individuals feel that they will be less effective without their moral outrage.

My own personal history includes times when I was beaten and betrayed. Sometimes, it takes a lot of personal self-discipline for me to turn the direction of my thoughts. It *is* possible, and I apply the methods that I share in this book and these following ideas:

- **Peace is found by turning to Higher Power.** Through prayer and spiritual activities we place our minds in another place—somewhere different from anger and hurt.

- **One way to turn to Higher Power is the process** *Wake Up In Gratitude.* In the morning, often my first conscious thought is: "Thank you, God, for this glorious day for love, excellent health, prosperity and happy surprises." I turn this day over to Higher Power.

- **Seek a Higher Power-centered approach.** I let go of my fearful thoughts such as "I don't know whether my writing is perfect enough." Instead, I approach each project or presentation with thoughts like this: "This is God's book for God's purposes. I'm participating."

- **Replace negative thoughts with empowering ones.** We need to *reduce* self-inflicted anger and self-inflicted stress. If we aren't mindful, we can increase our own personal pain. For example, someone I know, Nadine, got stuck in this thought: "I'll never trust anyone again. The perpetrator took my childhood away forever." With time, coaching and counseling, she learned to replace negative thoughts with empowering ones. She now tells herself, "The attack was in Chapter One of my life. I'm now in Chapter Two. I am now a strong adult and I can protect myself. Further, I can enjoy this day. And this moment."

Negative thoughts can be dealt with through various processes: journal writing, devoting time with a counselor, attending healing retreats, expressing feelings with a truly close friend, praying, meditating and other activities.

At some point many people find it necessary to replace their thoughts with more empowering thoughts like "Higher Power gives me some joyful moments each day. I can nurture myself with comforting moments with friends or when I'm alone with music, prayer, a warm bath..." An old saying emphasizes, "It's not what happens to us, it's how we respond."

- **Engaging in a healing process helps many of us to let go of painful feelings.** Many people join support groups, find solace in prayer, heal at weekend retreats, read spiritual texts, mediate, and/or devote time with a counselor.

- **Focus on solutions—a path towards peace of mind.** For example, I personally know people who take action to bring more peace into their lives. Sam (whose wife was brutally beaten and raped) now feels purpose and strength as he serves as a self-defense trainer. He said, "I cannot get justice nor can I act out feelings of vengeance on the unknown attacker. *But I can help these women here and now.*" Sam says that he is part of one solution for people confronted by the aftermath of violence.

- **Focus on the thought: "We can stand for something without being angry."** For example, I have friend, Tammy, who survived childhood sexual abuse. She told me about how she still has difficulties with her husband because she feels "the ghost of the perpetrator."

Frankly, I sometimes feel great anger when I see how Tammy struggles with trust issues and isolates herself. However, I choose to focus my thoughts on solutions. My response is to stand for something. Over the years, I have participated in helping women get scholarships so that they can get special training, including self-defense methods. The women can recover feelings of self-esteem and gain the capacity to take care of themselves if accosted.

My phrase, *We can stand for something without being angry*, implies taking action. Some people feel their role is to lobby for swifter, more extreme punishment of offenders. Others feel their role is to empower children and women with safety skills. The emphasis on *without being angry* notes that while taking action, we can go beyond relying only on moral outrage. Self-inflicted angry thoughts and self-inflicted stress can slow one down in fulfilling the action role towards solutions. I am emphasizing taking action *and* simultaneously turning to Higher Power for healing.

• **Open your awareness to the bigger picture.** My phrase is: *To forgive is not to pardon, it's to look at the bigger picture.* Looking at the bigger picture is a multi-faceted process. It involves our spiritual awareness, that we are spirits having a human experience. Our spirits are eternal, not our current feelings. There have been times when friends or family members have been judgmental and have withdrawn their loving-kindness from me. I have found it necessary to pause to see the bigger picture. Then, I saw that the other person was feeling hurt. His or her withdrawal of love was really a cry that asks for love. It is like the person is saying, "I have painful feelings, and I don't know what to do with them." So I stopped myself from falling into metaphorical chasm of anger. The point is: I continually strive to *not* return negativity for negativity. During painful times, I go elsewhere: to another friend, to comforting music and a warm bath, to an encouraging book or audio program. We can participate in activities that provide us with support and that help us release our painful feelings.

• **Ask for Higher Power's help.** Part of the bigger picture process is opening our awareness to the spiritual truth that we *can* heal—with help. For those times when pain obscures our view, prayer is helpful. Turn it over to God. One practice I have found useful is the God Box. When troubled, I write down the situation on a piece of paper and place it in my God Box. I say, "I turn this one over to you, God. Thanks for Your Help."

So turn it over to Higher Power. When we demonstrate willingness to let something go, and when we eventually feel better, it is a God-given miracle.

Remember to choose love and let go of fear.

* * *

Since I was speaking about fear, now we'll explore a big fear: the fear the arises when one feels called to make a *big change.* Along this line, here's an article by Dr. Kenneth Atchity:

GO FOR IT!
by Dr. Kenneth Atchity

Carl Jung: "Neurosis is no substitute for genuine suffering."

How many times have you felt as if you were hurtling toward a brick wall at 90 mph and someone supposedly dear to you gave you the advice, "Slow down!" or "Relax"? As many times as I'd been advised to slow down, I've wondered whether hitting the wall at thirty mph was truly preferable to hitting it at ninety m.p.h. If you're going to go splat, make it a complete splat! How else will you find out in time whether that wall is in fact, as you imagined, the secret door to your dreams?

My advice has to do with the speed and shape of your creative life—and about the wall that so often becomes a door. Your chosen speed and trajectory are precisely what distinguish you, a "Type C personality," from the others who are saying, "Relax."

If you're one of those blissful souls whose attitude is always perfect, who goes through life with an eternal smile of confidence, and who has never found it necessary to scream or cry, this advice is not for you. I wish I could say, through the years of my mid-life career transit that I've always been "up." The truth is, I've had to build my "upness," sometimes from what felt like scratch, nearly every day. I like to think it's because the life I've chosen requires me to do things I've never done before, things I wasn't always certain I could find a way of doing.

"What makes you an authority?"

Albert Einstein: "The punishment fate has given me for my hatred of authority is making me one."

Once upon a time I resigned my position as tenured professor of comparative literature at Occidental College in Los Angeles to pursue a new full-time career as free-lance writer, independent producer, literary manager, and entrepreneurial "story merchant." I exchanged a thirty-year "comfort horizon" (how much of the future you can envision as being covered by income-generating contracts presently in hand) for one that has ranged from a mere 24 hours to twelve months at the very best—normally hovering precariously between 45 and 90 days. When people told me that my mid-life career change was insane, I reminded them (and myself) of Salvador Dali's taunt: "The only difference between myself and a madman is that I am not mad." Regardless of how that struck my interrogator, it made me feel better.

My decision to resign from my tenured position became final in the middle of a December snowstorm in Montreal, where I was taking a leave of absence from Occidental College to supervise the production of the *Shades of Love* series of romantic comedies, which I had conceived and was producing, for Lorimar-Warner Brothers and Astral-Bellevue-Pathe. The decision followed on the heels of an event that brought the familiar sensation that everything happens for a reason: I was scheduled to play the "extra" part of a professor in one of the films, *Sincerely, Violet*, but had been delayed by a snowstorm. By the time I finally arrived on the set the scene had already been shot. I decided right then and there that I simply wasn't meant to play a professor even in fiction—that it was high time to resign my tenure. My appearance as an extra was rescheduled for the next day: I ended up playing a graphologist.

Although the incident in Montreal provoked immediate action, the decision had been a long time in the making, first conceived twelve years earlier while I was serving as Fulbright Professor at the University of Bologna. On Valentine's Day of that year, I received a telegram from the Occidental Dean of the Faculty informing me that I'd been granted tenure.

My immediate reaction to this news surprised me: I became depressed.

The depression continued for at least a year, compounded by my difficulty finding colleagues who could relate to such a bizarre reaction to what everyone else considered good news. I should have been ecstatic.

I finally figured it out for myself: I felt trapped, suffocated. My oldest recurrent nightmare as a child was of being suffocated by an enormous blanket not of my own weaving. Yes, the box I now found myself in was a comfortable one; but it was still a box—a golden cage. As much as I loved teaching, as much as I had succeeded at it, I was having trouble with the thought that for the next 39 years I'd be able to predict my schedule 12 months in advance. I felt that my life was spinning out of control, coming to an end, and that without knowing how, I had prematurely become a zombie.

I knew I had to escape.

I also knew I had something to contrast these dark feelings with, something that seemed trivial at the time. Even as a professor I couldn't keep my fingers out of various business pies. I ran a consulting company that specialized in helping writers perfect their work, that translated business documents from and into several languages, and that published and distributed poetry quarterlies. One day I received a most unexpected call "out of the blue"—from the State Department in Washington. A Yemeni diplomat was in the United States, wanting to meet with an American businessman and professor who was also a poet. It scares me to think how they found me, but they asked if I'd be willing to spend an afternoon with him.

He flew to Los Angeles and picked me up at my consulting office in Glendale. We spent a delightful afternoon talking about poetry, business, literature, and world affairs and were mutually impressed at the other's diverse interests. Early in the conversation he'd asked about my origins, and I'd explained my Lebanese/French Louisiana ancestry. He told me that I was following in the traditions of the Lebanese—"Phoenicians" originally—by being an "educated merchant," who believed in the poems and short stories I read and wrote enough to publish them. He pointed out that writing and publishing your own poetry and that of others was respectable behavior, and I couldn't help but think of the President of my College who'd once asked "what other entrepreneurial activities are you engaged in?" when he received a complaint from a fellow faculty member that I was distributing literary magazines. The word "entrepreneurial" sounded like "mudslinging" in his Ivy-League drawl.

At Occidental I'd created internships that allowed students to work at film studios, newspapers, and publishing companies "in the real world." As I lectured on creativity and writing on campuses throughout the country I began feeling more and more "dishonest" about the secure life I'd chosen for myself. I also realized two things:

I realized I hadn't really chosen to be a professor. I'd simply responded to job offers after finishing graduate school at Yale, accepting the most attractive one in a place that was most conducive to raising my young family. At the time, I also imagined that being a professor meant teaching all the time, without foreseeing the realities of committees, bureaucratic red tape, tenure battles that destroyed lives, and the ceaseless futility of campus politics.

Just how safe was the academic profession anyway? While tenure seemed a magical word for some people, I calculated that the economic realities were such that even tenure would not be immune should the College find itself in financial straits. The safety my colleagues valued so highly was, I decided, an illusion of security. I'd also never been comfortable in a costume, except maybe on Halloween. And being a professor, complete with tweed jackets and leather elbow pads, was costume. The word "uniform" was too painful to contemplate.

At one and the same time I realized that I preferred the illusion of freedom to the illusion of security. When I talked about my restlessness with novelist John Gardner, who at the time was editing my first book on Homer, he told me I was crazy; that I should remain a professor and do whatever else I wanted to do from that secure foundation. As a creative entrepreneur himself, he very wisely couldn't recommend his lifestyle when he compared it to mine.

So I hung on another year or so, satisfying my restlessness by founding and editing "off-campus" magazines: *CQ: Poetry and Art;* the interdisciplinary journal *DreamWorks* (dedicated to the study of dreams and the arts), with my colleague Marsha Kinder; and a Pasadena arts newspaper, *Follies*.

Then I had the good fortune to meet a man whose columns in *The Saturday Review* I'd enjoyed as a teenager, Norman Cousins.

No doubt a reflection of the mood I was in that year, I had found myself offering a course entitled "Literature and Death"; and, inspired by reading Norman's *Anatomy of an Illness*, invited him as a guest speaker. He accepted. During his presentation to my class, Norman used Ortega y Gasset's observation about intensity quoted on the opening page of this book: "I think the only immoral thing is for a being not to live every moment of his life with the utmost intensity."

Never having heard anyone else but myself cite these stirring words, I was stunned.

After class, I asked him to stop by my office for a minute on our way to the Faculty Club for lunch. I wanted to show Norman the plaque hanging above my desk, bearing the very words he'd quoted. He was moved. En route to lunch, I asked him if I could impose on a few moments of his time, at his convenience, to talk with him about "what I want to do when I grow up." He laughed, and asked me if I played tennis.

A few days later, to my pleasure and surprise, he called to ask if I could make the fourth in a doubles game. After a rousing set at Bea Arthur's private court in Mandeville Canyon, Norman listened to my achievements, dreams, and ambitions, and then offered me his advice.

"Whatever you do," he told me, "don't ever give up your diversity."

I couldn't believe my ears. All my previous advisers had consistently said the opposite. When I had first proposed the idea for *DreamWorks* to Paul Chance at *Psychology Today*, he'd responded with a long, thoughtful letter, criticizing the magazine's diversity, closing it with the words, "Find your niche, young man, find your niche." We proceeded with DreamWorks anyway, and it went on to win awards for its interdisciplinary "focus."

All my life I'd been seeking my niche among niches defined by others. Norman was advising me to create my own Type C niche, defining it with sufficient diversity to replace the suffocation response with excitement and hope.

His second suggestion threw me for even more of a loop. He told me that in his opinion the best place to exercise my particular talents and ambitions was the entertainment industry. When I replied that I knew nothing about that world, he recommended I read William Goldman's *Adventures in the Screen Trade* (Goldman's scripts and novels include *Marathon Man*, *Butch Cassidy and the Sundance Kid*, and *Magic*). I was ready to follow Norman's advice when, part way through Goldman's book, I encountered what the screenwriter-novelist called the "single most important fact" of the entire movie business: "NOBODY KNOWS ANYTHING." I realized immediately that I would be on a level playing field, and that I'd found my second career.

By the time I'd finished Goldman's book, I was convinced that I shouldn't go into my new career solely as a writer. For one thing, it would limit my ability to express other talents, like salesmanship, management, and entrepreneurial instincts. For another, writers have little leverage in this great big bad world until they're established. Unless they're lucky, they could wait forever to be recognized. I didn't want to rely on luck, and I didn't have forever. I realized I needed to learn enough about the industry to become a producer, having little idea then about what a producer does. At that point, serendipity again came to my assistance in the person of A. John Graves, who happened to be enrolled in my graduate course at California State College, Los Angeles on "Shakespeare's Ten Worst Plays."

Formerly an executive at NBC, John was now working as an independent producer. He approached me after class one night and asked if I'd ever considered a career in show business. I couldn't believe my ears. A few lunches later, I had the mentor I needed—and a desk full of contracts to read (My theory was that learning a new business would go faster if I started with the endpoint of a deal). I read every contract I could get my hands on. I'll never forget one that included, "Accounting terms shall be defined in such fashion as the Twentieth Century Fox accounting department shall define them at such time, if any, that litigation is entered into among the parties." Although I would wrestle with the concept many times in the future, I had just encountered for the first time what's known in "the biz" as "creative accounting."

Four years later, just after The New York Times had printed a full-page story about my Lorimar-Warner-Astral series of romantic comedies, I bumped into a mentor from my former life, Bart Giamatti, in the elevator of the New York City Yale Club.

"Atchity," he said, "What's this I hear about a professor of comparative literature producing romance movies?"

"What's this I hear about the President of Yale becoming the Baseball Commissioner?"

"Touché," he laughed.

Apparently I hadn't fallen too far from the tree.

In making the move from security to freedom, substituting an illusion I prefer for an illusion that was suffocating me, I had initiated a full-blown mid-life crisis. If

I'd taken the ten-question "stress test" two years after my resignation from Occidental, I would have set the record for "major life changes."

Within three years, I'd changed jobs, homes, cities, and spouse.

And my father died.

In the midst of one particular crisis in my brilliant new career, I found myself in San Francisco, at the home of dream therapist Gayle Delaney (*Living Your Dreams*). Gayle suggested that I incubate a dream to determine whether I truly thought I had within me the resources to continue along the course I'd set for myself.

That night I dreamed I found myself between two apparently equal serpents, and realized they were in the process of devouring me. But they didn't. I woke up elated.

"What do you think the serpents represent?" Gayle asked the next morning.

"My problems? My conflicting motivations?" I thought about it, deciding that they must relate to my theory of the two parts of the mind being in constant war with each other. By the time we'd worked it out, I realized that the dream was directly related to my lifelong fascination, as a student and teacher of mythology, with Mercury's caduceus—the flowering rod, plume, and serpents (although some representations show only one serpent, I've always favored the ones with two).

The snakes in my dream were the Past and the Future, with my own personal skills between them in the Present, barely managing to keep me upright. The Past was trying to pull me back, the Future, with all its fears and anxieties, was trying to devour my energy. But I was safe in the Present because the focal point of safety lies in the centered self that has learned by mastering itself to master the world. No wonder I would come to love Eckhart Tolle's *The Power of Now*.

As a student of Homer's *Odyssey*, I recognized that the mythic origins of the dream were related to the Greek concept of techné, the protean virtue of Athena and Hermes (Mercury), whose mortal counterpart is Homer's hero Odysseus. As Odysseus was able to vanquish the serpentine monsters encountered on his embattled journey to Ithaca, I would be able to master the draconian serpents threatening me from both sides.

The dream was reminding me, in other words, that fighting dragons was my natural strength. No wonder, despite my high anxiety, I was essentially content with my decision. My contentment had reached its height one blizzardy day on a flight between Montreal and Toronto, when the prospect of the plane going down in the storm didn't concern me enough to make me look up from the script I was editing. At the time, we were still shooting one film in Montreal; but were already in post-production on another film at Pathé's sound lab in Toronto. A "final mix" was scheduled that night (where the music is added to the film's sound effects). Everyone thought I should skip the mix because of the weather, but I was determined to master every detail of my new career, and went to Dorval Airport. Once there, I discovered that Air Canada had canceled its flight to Toronto because of the storm. But a smaller, prop driven airliner was scheduled to leave in ten minutes. I decided to take it, ignoring the fear of flying I'd always previously experienced.

As the plane lumbered through the snowstorm it occurred to me that the possibility that I might die on this flight didn't disturb me. I was living my dream, and dying in the middle of my dream would be a happy death. In her studies of death and the dying, Elizabeth Kubler-Ross found that people "are not afraid of death per se, but of the incompleteness of their lives, of dying prematurely."

Up there in the blizzard, on that plane, I felt my life was complete. And I realized I'd have to expand my dream in order to give me reason to continue living with this wonderful sense of fulfillment.

I began to accept that my view of success wasn't about garnering achievements so much as about achieving (in the words of Robert Browning, "Ah, but a man's reach should exceed his grasp, /Or what's a heaven for?"); and that this view made me different from many of the people who, along the way, came to me for jobs, consultations, or conversations about "how to do what you did." Listening to them, consulting with them, I realized that it was product, not process, that turned them on. I began to see that whether they are salespeople or athletes, writers or inventors, builders, proprietors of boutiques, or entrepreneurs, Type C personalities are quite different from others. They're in love with the words, "Go for it."

People tell me that it "took a lot of courage" to resign the total security of a tenured position. The comment sounded alien to me at first, and then started to trouble me more and more. I've always taken pride in doing something good, and "courage" sounds very good. At one point early in my new career, at Marsha Sinetar's suggestion (author of the inspiring *Do What You Love, The Money Will Follow*), Dr. Joyce Brothers and her television crew came to interview me about career change. As usual, I was under enormous pressure, but I did my best to talk sensibly about why I made my own transition and what it felt like to be in the middle of it. Dr. Joyce kept saying it was "courageous," and I kept changing the subject to my worries about "the wolf at the door." But when the program aired a few months later, I had to admit even I was impressed with how my story sounded. One of my fellow interviewees was a hairdresser who'd gone after her medical degree in psychiatry at the age of forty something. Earning that credential had allowed her to exchange listening to clients for $25 an hour to listening to them for $125 an hour. Another was a man in his eighties who was just receiving his law degree—his fifth career change. He recounted his experience on registration day.

"The young man behind me in line finally asked, 'Sir, excuse me for asking but what are you doing in this line?'"

"What line should I be in?" the octogenarian had answered.

I could see now why what I had done sounded courageous to others. But I didn't feel courageous. Instead, on many mornings and afternoons and especially evenings when I had absolutely no idea how I could continue for another hour, I felt certain I'd made a gigantic mistake. Had I foreseen what it would cost me in every aspect of my life, I told myself, I might never have undertaken my new career. Visualizing the future is one thing. Seeing it in actuality would have discouraged me.

Instead of "courage" the word I came to use was "challenge." I needed to feel challenged, needed to challenge myself. My career transit was a necessity, not a luxury, keeping my sense of "self" intact. Did I have the strength and stamina to face the unfamiliar adversities I had chosen for myself? And to be called, in the process, "self centered," "selfish," "irresponsible," and "crazy"?

Sophocles: "It's a terrible thing to look upon your troubles and to realize that you yourself and no one else are responsible for them."

Let's admit that it takes courage to express your Type C personality (the Type B alcoholic who LOVES his creative work!)—to live with the consequences of your decision to be yourself—whatever you conceive that self to be. It takes courage to stand apart from all the "normal" people out there who criticize and raise their eyebrows, wondering why you're so crazy (while they wonder, to themselves, why they can't be a little more like you).

Even more, it takes courage to stand against the enemy within: the normal person inside you, shaped by your parents and the Society of the Non weird, who spends his every waking effort trying to stop you from doing something as insane as quitting a high paying, secure position to pursue your idiosyncratic need for freedom, creativity, and self definition.

Career transition isn't recommended for the overly critical or for those who need security. It's for those who know that the ultimate challenge lies in the self realization that comes only when you pit skills beyond your present imagining against the relentless resourcefulness of a world of troubles. Theodore Roosevelt was such a man. He said:

It is not the critic who counts, not the man who points out how the strong man stumbled, or where the doer of deeds could have done them better. The credit belongs to the man who is actually in the arena; whose face is marred by dust and sweat and blood; who strives valiantly; who errs and comes up short again and again; who knows the great enthusiasms; the great devotions; and spends himself in a worthy cause; who, at the best, knows in the end the triumph of high achievement; and who, at the worst, if he fails, at least fails while daring greatly, so that his place shall never be with those cold and timid souls who know neither victory nor defeat.

Roosevelt makes "risk taking" and "being creative" sound glamorous to those who haven't gone for it. He, like those who have gone for their dreams, knew better. No one in his right mind would encourage anyone over the age of 25 to sacrifice security for the uncharted territory of a new career—unless the idea was one they came up with themselves.

But if you feel a strong need to change, if you're one of those people who long to live the creative life of a professional writer, this advice might help you chart that new territory. Francisco de Goya complained that, "the sleep of reason produces monsters." Deal with the monsters of your imagination and you will enter with joy into the undiscovered country down the road not previously taken.

The ultimate investment is investing in yourself, by designing a life around your unique interests. Everyone might tell you that this is the way to happiness, but very few people will encourage you to pursue such selfishness. Even fewer pursue it for themselves. Those who do are the ones who make a difference. When creative career change is successful, it leads to fulfillment. But what about when it's not successful? As you get into it, you quickly begin to realize that "success" is ephemeral. Not simply because change is tough, but because even the word "success" must be redefined in order to continue being useful. I didn't feel successful after having produced my first films, but I felt very successful while producing them. Success is doing not having done. That's what St. Catherine of Siena meant when she observed, "All the way to heaven is heaven."

Aside from suffocation, my greatest fear in life had always been feeling that I would come to feel that my energies weren't being challenged, that my time on earth was being wasted. I'd reacted strongly to the poignancy of former President Lyndon Johnson's telltale comment: "To hunger for use, and to go unused, that is the greatest hunger of all." The person who engages in a career transition has made the conscious decision to create that need to be used and useful. He is following in the footsteps of George Bernard Shaw who wrote forty-one of his fifty-two produced plays after age 45, *Pygmalion* at age 57, *Saint Joan* at age 67, and *Buoyant Billions* at age 91. Shaw wrote:

This is the true joy in life, the being used for a purpose recognized by yourself as a mighty one; the being thoroughly worn out before you are thrown on the scrap heap; the being a force of Nature instead of a feverish selfish little clod of ailments and grievances complaining that the world will not devote itself to making you happy.

Everyone's first career is an accident. Your next career, the child of your choice, is your mighty purpose that makes life worth living. Go for it!

Dr. Kenneth Atchity is a literary manager, producer, editor, and author, whose latest book, *The Messiah Matrix*, was the first to predict the election of an Argentine Jesuit

pope (www.messiahmatrix.com). He can be reached: Atchity@storymerchant.com.

This article is adapted from his *How to Quit Your Day Job and Live Out Your Dreams* (available on Amazon.com at http://amzn.to/1efsAAG).

* * * * * *

Topic #8
Book Four: Enjoy Life's Many Facets
Get More Done—Faster and Better for True Success

Would you like to get more done and feel better doing it?

Working with clients, I emphasize: "Momentum Makes Miracles." We'll use the C.A.N. process:

C – clear distractions

A – arrange "the start"

N – nurture great timing

1. Clear distractions

Cheryl feels squeezed by responsibilities both at work and with family. She gets into the habit of doing two things at once. She'll talk on the phone while sitting with her son and playing a game of checkers. She'll write an email while responding to a phone call at work.

Recent research has demonstrated that multi-tasking is NOT doing two things at once. It is really "rapid starts and stops." That is, if one is typing an email and talking on the phone at the same time, one's brain is starting to type the email and quickly stopping one's attention to the phone call. And then one is quickly taking attention off the email and putting it back to the phone conversation. Several researchers conclude that it is NOT more efficient to do two things at once. The person is actually using up more brain energy than necessary. Actual lab results show that the person who "multi-tasks" actually does the two things with less precision and less effectiveness. Not good.

"Clearing distractions" can be as simple as turning off a chime that rings each time email arrives in your inbox. For many people, that chime interrupts their train of thought. Then they may lose their momentum. Worse: they have to gear up (and lose time doing it) to get back to where they were in the project.

Another example: Much of my work is creative so I have times in the day in which I turn off the ringer on my cell phone. I do NOT want to have my creativity and my momentum on a project to be interrupted.

2. Arrange "the start"

Inspiration usually comes during work rather than before it.
– Madeleine L'Engle

As a professional writer, I frequently press on and start working on a writing project no matter how I feel. Several times a month, I start writing and I immediately do not like the first few paragraphs. I think, "This is not good enough." But I press on anyway. Often, five minutes into continuing my writing, I finally start to see material that I actually like. As top author Madeleine L'Engle advises: Inspiration usually comes during work rather than before it.

So my point is: Simply start. Do NOT wait for inspiration. Do NOT wait to "feel like doing" the task.

Do you need to make headway on your taxes paperwork? Simply start by laying the folders out on your desk. Just concentrate on that small step to just start. Consider using the words "Just Start" as a form of mantra to get you going.

I keep a log of the writing I complete during the day. I focus on my phrase: Keep Score and Achieve More. I just start by looking at the log and seeing yesterday's progress.

3. Nurture great timing

Find your "Best Moments" during the day. For me, the first moments after awakening are "prime time." I avoid answering email at this time. I avoid calling a friend. I simply sit down and start writing. Often as I'm waking up, my subconscious mind is serving up new ideas and good ideas that I want to immediately type into my current writing project (like this article). My family knows that I will not come down and eat first when I wake up in the morning. I often start writing and after completing some work—then I'll take a break and have breakfast.

That's my process. Find your own Best Moments.

Secondly, for your great timing, effectively incorporate breaks in your schedule. With an appropriate break, you'll be surprised how refreshed you feel and how much momentum you'll have on a project upon your return.

For example, one of my friends has been away from creative work for a number of months. Then she rearranged her schedule and cleared some time. Suddenly, she's now writing a book, writing songs and drawing illustrations for two children's books. She calls it "a miracle." Truly her time away from creativity was, for her, a revving up time. At this point, it's time for her to nurture her momentum. Perhaps, she'll limit some of her social activities so that she can take advantage of her momentum and churn out a lot of creative work.

Remember: **Momentum Makes Miracles.**

* * *

To really nurture your momentum, it helps to focus on the *critical few* instead of the mediocre many. To be successful, many of us need to help others buy (that's an empowering viewpoint of "selling"). Now, I'll share C.J. Hayden's insights on this process.

What Really Makes People Buy?
by C.J. Hayden

It's the ultimate question, isn't it? You work hard at marketing to make contact with potential clients. Then you work even harder to get a chance speak with them about what you have to offer. But how do you actually get them to hire you? The answers may not be what you think.

1. Know-Like-and-Trust Factor – When making a buying decision about professional services, the number one factor clients consider is how much they know, like, and trust you. It's more important than how much you charge or even how much they need you. What clients are asking is: How much contact have they had with you? Did they recognize your name beforehand? Are you credible as a competent professional? Were you referred by someone they know?

You can influence this factor by focusing your marketing efforts on meeting clients through networking, referrals, and public speaking. If you haven't had prior contact with prospective clients and weren't referred, give them copies of any published work or media coverage you have, and provide them with client testimonials. Be prepared to stay in touch over a period of time so they can get to know you better.

2. Match between your offer and their needs – If you pass the first test of seeming credible and trustworthy, potential clients next look at how closely what you offer matches what they are looking for. Do they have a pressing need for your services? Do they understand exactly what it is that you provide? Do they grasp the benefits of working with you?

The best way to address this issue is to ask plenty of questions. The more you can find out about what the client needs, the better you can explain specifically how you can help. The biggest mistake professionals make when selling themselves is to offer themselves as a solution when they don't yet know the problem. Be sure also to communicate the benefits of hiring you—not just what you do, but what the client gets as a result of what you do.

3. Justifying the purchase – An often neglected component of the buying decision is whether the client will be able to justify spending money on your services to their spouse, boss, board of directors, or even themselves. In business environments, this is critical. The purchaser must be able to support their decision to hire you with verifiable facts. When selling to consumers, keep in mind there may be a naysayer in the background who will need to be convinced of your value.

Give your prospects the evidence they need to justify your value to others. Provide statistics or examples of results achieved, money saved, or performance improved in your former projects. Share a case study, your client list, or a portfolio of your successes. Help them find the language they need to reassure everyone involved that hiring you is the most practical solution available to the problem at hand.

4. Price vs. budget – The last element prospective clients consider is the price. Yes, cost is important, but if they trust you, your offer is a good match for what they need, and they can justify hiring you, then the only significant issue about the price is whether they can find the money.

Suggest ways they can evaluate their investment in you, such as comparing it to the cost of doing nothing, measuring it against another more expensive solution, or weighing the drawbacks of doing it themselves. For corporate clients, help them look for unused funds in other budget categories or propose the project for the next budget cycle. With consumers and small businesses, how much they can afford depends on where else they are spending their money. If funds are tight, suggest other expenses that your services might replace or reduce, offer a payment plan, or accept credit cards.

The next time you're wondering why a sale isn't going through, check how you're doing on each of these four factors. See if you can discover the missing ingredients that will convince the client to buy.

C.J. Hayden, MCC, CPCC, is the bestselling author of *Get Clients Now!*, *The One-Person Marketing Plan Workbook*, and over 400 articles. C.J. is a business coach and teacher who helps entrepreneurs get clients, get strategic, and get things done. Her company, Wings for Business, specializes in serving self-employed professionals and solopreneurs.

A popular speaker and workshop leader, C.J. has presented hundreds of programs on marketing and entrepreneurship to corporate clients, professional associations, and small businesses. She has taught marketing for John F. Kennedy University, Mills College, the U.S. Small Business Administration, and SCORE. She contributes regularly to dozens of magazines and websites, including Home Business, RainToday, Salesopedia, and About.com.

WEBSITE: www.getclientsnow.com
CONTACT: info@getclientsnow.com   (877) 946-4722

* * *

To be successful we need to be the leader of our own lives. Many of us also need to lead others to accomplish big goals. Now, I'll share Mark Sanborn's insights.

The 7 Disciplines of a Successful Leader
by Mark Sanborn

Fellow professional speaker Scott Ginsberg once asked me, "What do you do each day to assure your ongoing success?" I thought it was one of the best questions I've ever been asked.

For over 25 years, I've considered what activities have given me the biggest payback on my investment of time and expertise as a leader. The biggest challenge of leadership isn't being successful; it is being successful over the long run. Longevity trumps the temporary, and requires daily disciplines.

At different times in your business, there will be different things you need to do, but these seven activities—when done daily—will stack the odds in your favor for long-term success.

1. Capture ideas: Each day, read, observe, contemplate and capture ideas that will be relevant to your audience and useful in your speaking, writing, coaching and consulting. Reading broadly and eclectically develops intellectual bandwidth. If you read only what others are reading, you will likely lack the ingredients for true originality.

2. Sell something: While getting out and making sales calls is always a good idea for staying in touch with customers, that's not only what I mean. Ideas have consequences, and leaders go beyond simple telling to selling. They know what matters and they make it matter to others. Whether a needed change or a suggestion for improvement, sell the ideas that matter most.

3. Build and deepen relationships: People rarely change or improve outside of relationship. When people are asked about the leaders who have made the biggest difference in their lives, they first site warmth and personal connection. Leadership is about making connections and keeping them.

Great leaders get results by focusing as much or more on the relational as the transaction, and the relational is born out of genuine concern. When was the last time you called or emailed a colleague or client with no other motive than checking in on them and their well-being?

4. Create: Leadership is an art as well as a science. Your vision will be richer because of creativity, not stenography. Write a story, post a blog, send a tweet, but do something that requires imagination. Your creative muscle is developed with use, and unless it is being built over time, it won't be available to you when needed.

5. Improve something: Look at every aspect of your performance and your business. Find something you can tweak, improve or overhaul for maximum impact and effectiveness. Pick one area of your business operations to scrutinize and improve with your team each month.

6. Learn a new idea: Capturing ideas for your content development is different from looking for new ideas on how to live your life better. Learning also keeps you from stagnating—personally and professionally. My longtime friend and futurist Dan Burrus, picks one new skill to learn each year.

7. Enjoy: Make the most of each moment and the moments will become a life well lived. You can enjoy the successes and even the setbacks, if you look at them as learning opportunities. Don't only do what needs to be done; make it a habit to do those things you really enjoy. Have fun. As the legendary Michael Jackson (not the singer, but the Brit known as the Beer Hunter) said, "Moderation is

good, as long as it is in moderation."

What will you do each day to assure your ongoing success? And what would you add to this list?

Mark Sanborn is the president of Sanborn & Associates, Inc., an idea lab for leadership development.

In addition to his experience leading at a local and national level, he has written or co-authored 8 books and is the author of more than two dozen videos and audio training programs on leadership, change, teamwork and customer service. He has presented over 2400 speeches and seminars in every state and a dozen countries.

Mark is a member of the prestigious Speakers Roundtable, 20 of the top speakers in the world today. Mark holds the Certified Speaking Professional (CSP) from the National Speakers Association and is a member of the Speaker Hall of Fame (CPAE).

The author of 8 books, Mark's book, *The Fred Factor: How Passion in Your Work and Life Can Turn the Ordinary Into the Extraordinary* was an international bestseller and has sold over 2 million copies. The sequel, *Fred. 2.0*, was released in March of 2013.

He is the leading authority on turning ordinary into extraordinary and is in demand as a speaker, author and advisor to leaders.

Contact Mark at www.MarkSanborn.com

* * *

Any discussion of success will include goal-setting. Now, I'll share Rebecca Morgan's surprising ideas on effective goal-*achieving*.

Don't Focus on Reaching Your Goals
by Rebecca Morgan, CSP, CMC

Traditional advice is to set stretch goals, a tad beyond what you believe you can achieve, then celebrate when you've achieved them.

I have a different perspective. Don't focus on if you achieve them. Set audacious goals and look at who you have to become in order to achieve what you previously thought was not possible. Then celebrate your new habits, attitude or wisdom garnered from stretching way beyond what you thought was possible, even if you didn't make the goal.

A gal pal shared that her shy, 7-year-old daughter was setting out to sell Girl Scout cookies in her neighborhood. She asked her daughter how many she thought she could sell. "Eight boxes" was the response. My friend felt her daughter was shooting a bit low, and said, "How about trying to sell 16 boxes?" The little girl shook her head that she'd try.

Off she went to knock on neighbors' doors. Soon she burst back into the house, "Mommy, I've sold 22 boxes!" She had to overcome her shyness and she accomplished way beyond she originally thought. She's now sold 160 boxes!

Many years ago, late on Sunday night at the end of a 3-day intense personal-growth weekend, we were asked to share how many guests we'd be bringing to the graduation night 2 days hence. A few of the 150 in attendance raised their hands and we heard, "One, " "Three" "Five" or a rare "Ten"—at which point there was much cheering and applause for someone so willing to commit to a large number aloud. I thought, "If I got my best friend, her husband and my mother, I could get 3, so maybe I should say 5." Then something came over me. I saw that it wasn't about actually achieving bringing the number of guests you'd publicly declared, but more about the growth it would involve to go way beyond what I thought was possible.

I stood and declared "One hundred." I don't remember, but I'm imagining there were gasps.

The next morning I arose early to see how close I could get to 100. I found I had to alter the invitation from just "please come" or "I'd appreciate your being there" to "It would mean a lot to me if you were there" then expounding on why this person was important to me and what the weekend learning's had meant to me. I dialed and dialed and had conversations with people I hadn't spoken to in a while. I sincerely told them what had transpired for me that weekend and invited them to share the celebration.

By the end of the second day, the last person confirmed minutes before I left for the celebration. I had 22 people show up.

My lesson was that most of us aim low—I certainly know I did. There's a lot of cultural pressure to achieve what one has publicly promised. And we celebrate achieving even modest goals as if they were huge stretches. There's typically no acknowledgement for not achieving goals, even when what was accomplished went way beyond the initial safe goal. Safe goals save face; stretch goals help you achieve a bit more, but audacious goals create shifts in who you are.

In my calls, I had to dig deep and share from a place I hadn't before with many of my contacts. I saw how our relationship then deepened not only in that conversation, but forever. I liked the shift as we were being less superficial and more intimate in sharing things that truly mattered.

So see if you can shift to celebrating who you've become when you make an outrageous, unreasonable, "unachievable" goal. You may find you not only like the person who emerges as you make every attempt to accomplish what you set out, but that your relationships improve—plus you'll most likely achieve more.

Rebecca L. Morgan, CSP, CMC, specializes in creating innovative solutions for customer service challenges. She's appeared on 60 Minutes, Oprah, the Wall Street Journal, National Public Radio and *USA Today*. Rebecca is the bestselling author of 25 books, including *Calming Upset Customers* and *Professional Selling*. She is an exemplary resource who partners with you to accomplish high ROI on your strategic customer service projects. For information on her services, books, and resources, or for permission to repost or reprint this article, contact her at
408/998-7977, Rebecca@RebeccaMorgan.com, http://www.RebeccaMorgan.com

* * *

Have you noticed that many of us get so caught up with setting and achieving big goals that we're stressed out?

Consider uplifting goals (or focus-areas) which include: nurture yourself and create connection with people you encounter each day.

Along this line, I'll now share Allen Klein's insights about inspiring people to enjoy connection through shared laughter.

Laughter is the shortest distance between two people.
- Victor Borge

HOW TO BE FUNNY WITHOUT TELLING JOKES:
Eight Humor Tips for Speakers
by Allen Klein, MA, CSP

For sixteen years, I have been showing audiences how to find humor in not-so-funny stuff. Thousands of people have laughed a lot in my presentations yet I don't tell jokes. Below are some ways I get people to laugh. And you can, too.

1 - Set the Scene for Laughter
If you want to lighten up your program, you might want to let the audience know this, even before you say one word. Project some lighthearted visuals as the audience is entering the room. Play some copyright-free uplifting music as they enter. Or, add some humor to your presentation title or program description. My bio, for example, has my list of accomplishments, playfully followed by "His mother is very proud of him."

2 - Poke Fun at Yourself
Again, even before you open your mouth, you can show the audience that you don't take yourself too seriously by adding some playful things about you in your introduction. I, for example, have the introducer tell the audience that I am the author of seven books which have sold well over 30 copies. Then the person corrects their mistake and says, "Oops, that's 300,000 copies."

3 - Get a Laugh with a Prop
It has been said that 80% of what people learn is visual. If this is true, then speakers need to enhance their talks with something to visually illustrate what they are saying. A prop

is a great way to do this because it not only makes your message memorable but it can also get a laugh. Among other things, I use balloons to illustrate how people can let go of their stress; an inflatable globe to illustrate how we often carry the world around on our shoulders; and a plastic hammer which I use to hit myself on the head when I goof up. All make a point and all get a laugh.

4 - Your Humor Stories

Open your humor eyes and ears and look and listen for the funny things that happen all around you. Families are an especially good resource for finding humor stories. Not too long ago, my Mom, who will be 93-years-old this year, told me an incident which I have now incorporated into my opening. Every time she goes to the doctor, she hires a van service to take her there and back. One late afternoon it didn't show up to take her home. Since the doctor had to close the office for the day, he suggested that she wait for the van in the pizza parlor next door. After waiting a long time without the van arriving, my Mom went up to the counter and asked, "Do you deliver?" When the man behind the counter replied, "Of course, we do. We're a pizza place." My Mom said, "Great. Then I'd like a pepperoni pizza and I'd like to go with it."

5 - Borrow Some Witty Words

While waiting for your own humor-related stories to appear, you might want to borrow some funny short quotes for famous folk to lighten up your talks. Quotation books, the TV, newspapers, and magazines such as *Reader's Digest* are great resources for locating great quotes. Since I frequently speak to hospice groups, Woody Allen's comments about death and dying are appropriate. My favorite, "There are worse things in life than death. Have you ever spent an evening with an insurance salesman?"

6 - Collect Audience Anecdotes

Sometimes audiences say the funniest things. When they do write it down. It could be a big laugh in your next presentation. For years, I've been asking audiences, "How do you spell relief?" My answer is "L-A-U-G-H". Then one day a woman in the back row called out, "D-I-V-O-R-C-E." It got a huge laugh for her that day and continues to get a laugh for me when I retell it.

7 - Make it Relevant

One final word about using humor in your presentations. Make sure it is relevant. Amusing an audience for the sake of getting a laugh might be ideal for a stand-up comedian or an after-dinner humorist but it's probably not OK for most speakers. If your humor doesn't make a point or have a purpose don t use it!

8 - The Bottom Line

For non-humorists, some of the ideas presented here may seem too frivolous for your subject matter. Nevertheless, I would still encourage you to seek some way of upping the entertainment value of your talks because it might also increase what you charge. As Steve Allen once noted, "People will pay more to be entertained than educated."

Allen Klein, aka "Mr. Jollytologist", is an award-winning professional speaker who shows audiences worldwide how to find and use humor to deal with changes, challenges, and not-so-funny stuff. He is a recipient of a Lifetime

Achievement Award from the Association for Applied and Therapeutic Humor, a Toastmaster's Communication and Leadership Award, a Certified Speaking Professional designation from the National Speaker's Association and a Hunter College (NYC) Hall of Fame honoree. Klein is also the best-selling author of such books *as The Healing Power of Humor, Learning to Laugh When You Feel Like Crying,* and *The Art of Living Joyfully*, among others. Contact: humor@allenklein.com or www.allenklein.com

A FINAL WORD AND THE SPRINGBOARD TO YOUR DREAMS

Congratulations on your efforts with this book.

To gain more value from this book, be sure to go through it and develop your own To Do List. Take some action. Any action towards improving skills and enlarging your life is helpful. I often say, "Better than zero."

One of my popular articles at my blog www.BeHeardandBeTrusted.com has the title: *"Enjoy the Best in Life (Your Power in Facing Risk)"*

Here is the text of that article:

Do you miss that feeling of joy and anticipation that you had in earlier years? Remember feeling excited about things in your life? You can have that experience again. How? Connect with this idea:

Face risk and disappointment to feel alive!

I have a couple of friends who have a disheartening response to this question: "How are things going?" Their reply: "Same old, same old."

How sad.

Instead, I invite you to consider having a Milestone Binder. You'll take action and try new activities—and then note your experiences in your Milestone Binder.

You note things that you try for the first time.

In my own Milestone Binder, I have these entries (which have taken place over the years):

The First Time ...

1) directing a feature film
2) auditioning for a commercial
3) performing as lead singer of a band

4) addressing an audience of 719 people
5) teaching MBA students at Stanford University
6) having a face-to-face meeting with a literary agent
7) helmet-diving

To put it in few words, I've faced risk often and sometimes I've failed.

I've learned that you need to keep swinging the bat in order to have some home runs.

I've also learned **three important strategies (the 3 Rs)** related to facing risk and disappointment.

Strategy #1: Reduce the downside

When I do a project, I make sure that the budget is NOT excessive and does not bring down the company. In fact, I have a couple of projects going at one time because I know some projects fail to bring in a preferred income. As a couple of millionaires have said, "You only have to be right 51% of the time."

Strategy #2: Rehearse

Before any first time event, rehearse. In fact, I encourage my clients and graduate students to use this practice: Any time you feel fear, rehearse.

Strategy #3: Regroup with a "Celebrate Someone Disagrees" Celebration

I remember when my second book came out. One of my close friends trashed it. In my mind, I had this thought: "Well, I didn't write it for you."

No matter what value you bring with a project, someone is not going to like it. Instead of letting that stop me, I realize that resistance and dislike for any project just happens.

So I invite you to have a "Celebrate Someone Disagrees" Celebration.

For example, someone close to me had her book rejected by a committee at a top publishing company. I said, "I'm with you. It hurts. And tell me when you might want to celebrate."

"Celebrate?" she asked.

"Yes, celebrate your courage to put something out into the world. Celebrate your courage and persistence to get something done! And finally celebrate that if you don't put anything into the world then no one will disagree about the value of the project. I call it 'Celebrate Someone Disagrees.'"

My friend got into the swing of things and said, "Sushi! I want to celebrate with sushi!"

Great!

In summary, to feel those moments of triumph and feeling proud of yourself, you'll need to face risk and disappointment.

People who succeed face adversity. They keep going. The one thing they avoid is the regret of not having taken action.

I do not regret the things I've done, but those I did not do.
– Rory Cochrane

Enjoy the best in life. Face risk and disappointment and **feel alive!**

* * *

Please consider gaining special training through my coaching (phone and in-person), workshops, presentations and Top Five Group Elite Video Training.

As you continue to work toward expanding your financial abundance and fulfillment in life, you are likely to come up against some tough situations. To be supportive I've written a number of books...

- Darkest Secrets of Charisma
- Darkest Secrets of Persuasion and Seduction Masters: How to Protect Yourself and Turn the Power to Good
- Darkest Secrets of Negotiation Masters
- Darkest Secrets of Making a Pitch to the Film and Television Industry
- Darkest Secrets of Film Directing
- Darkest Secrets of the Film and Television Industry Every Actor Should Know
- Darkest Secrets of Spiritual Seduction Masters
- Success Secrets of Rich, Smart and Powerful People: How You Can Use Leverage for Business Success

See my blog at
www.BeHeardandBeTrusted.com

The best to you,
Tom
Tom Marcoux,
America's Communication Coach
Motion Picture Director, Actor, Producer, Screenwriter
P.S. See **Free Chapters** of Tom Marcoux's 23 books at http://amzn.to/ZiCTRj

Titles include:
Be Heard and Be Trusted
Nothing Can Stop You This Year
Truth No One Will Tell You
10 Seconds to Wealth
Your Secret Charisma
Wake Up Your Spirit to Prosperity
— and more.
(For coaching, reach Tom Marcoux at tomsupercoach@gmail.com)

EXCERPT FROM
DARKEST SECRETS OF PERSUASION AND SEDUCTION MASTERS: HOW TO PROTECT YOURSELF AND TURN THE POWER TO GOOD

by Tom Marcoux, America's Communication Coach
Copyright Tom Marcoux

... Now, I am in my 40's, with gray in my hair, and for 27 years I have been taking action to protect people.

And now is the time for me to protect you with the Countermeasures I reveal in this book.

Every human being needs to be able to
break the trance that a Manipulator creates.
You need to make good decisions
so you are safe and you keep growing
—and you are not cut down and crippled.

This Secrets material is so intense that I first released it only with the counterbalance of my most energizing and uplifting books, *Nothing Can Stop You This Year!* and *10 Seconds to Wealth: Master the Moment Using Your Divine Gifts.*

An interviewer asked me: "Who can be the Manipulator?"

A co-worker, a boss, a salesperson, someone you're dating, and someone you think is a friend.

Now is the time—this very minute—for me to write this book to protect you.

I must speak the truth.

These Darkest Secrets of "persuasion masters" are ...

Wait a minute! Let's say it plainly: These are the Darkest Secrets of masters of manipulation. Throughout this book, I will call these people what they are: Manipulators.

Dictionary.com defines "manipulate" as "To influence or manage shrewdly or deviously.... To tamper with or falsify for personal gain."

In this book, we will look on a manipulator as one who deviously influences someone with no concern about that person's well-being, and who causes harm to that person.

Here is the first Darkest Secret:

Darkest Secret #1:
Manipulators Make You Hurt
and Then Offer the Salve.

Manipulators would invite you to go out in the sun for hours and then sell you the salve to soothe your burns. The problem is that we don't notice that this is what they're doing.

For example, you're considering the purchase of a house. A Manipulator asks the question, "So, where would you put your TV?" This question is designed to put you into a trance.

Dictionary.com defines "trance" as "a half-conscious state, seemingly between sleeping and waking, in which ability to function voluntarily may be suspended." Let's condense this: in a trance you may not be able to function freely.

Here is the second Secret:

Darkest Secret #2:
Manipulators Put You into a Trance.

To protect yourself, you must learn to use Countermeasures to Break the Trance.

All the Countermeasures (actions you can take to break the trance) in this book will make you stronger and more capable of protecting yourself.

Now, we'll view the third Secret:

Darkest Secret #3:
Manipulators Care Nothing for You and Human Decency:
They'll lie, cheat, and do whatever they need to do so they win—but their charm masks all this.

Let's return to the example of a Manipulator selling you a house. A Manipulator does not pause for an instant to see if you can truly afford the new house. The Manipulator would neglect to mention that you will not only have your mortgage payment of $900. There will be additional costs: home repairs, property tax, water, electricity, homeowner's insurance, and more. The Manipulator only emphasizes what he or she knows you want to hear: "Look! $900 is better than the $1500 you're paying for rent, which is just going down the toilet. And the $900 is an investment."

Let's go back to **Secret #1:**
Manipulators make you hurt and then offer the salve.

The Manipulator has you feeling good about the solution (salve) and feeling bad about your current life situation.

How? A Manipulator will make you hurt through questions such as:
- What bothers you about paying $1500 a month for rent? (The Manipulator will use a derisive tone when he says the word rent.)
- What is not smart about paying rent on someone else's house instead of investing in your own house?
- How do you feel about your children walking in the neighborhood where you live now?

Do you see how these questions are designed to make you hurt enough so that you'll buy?

An interviewer asked me, "Tom, aren't these good arguments for purchasing a house?"

"What we're looking at is the *intention* of the influencer," I replied. "Let's look at our definition of a manipulator as one who deviously influences someone with no concern about that person's well-being, and who causes harm to that person. If the person truly cannot afford the house, he or she will be harmed by buying it. If the manipulator conceals the truth, the manipulator is doing harm. That's the important difference."

Some friends of mine are ethical and helpful real estate agents who truthfully reveal the whole situation and help the purchaser achieve her own goals.

In this book, we are talking about another type of person; that is, unethical Manipulators.

* * *

In any given moment, we need to remember the tactics Manipulators use. We will focus on the word D.A.R.K. so you can remember details easily and protect yourself from Manipulators.

D — Dangle something for nothing
A — Alert to scarcity
R — Reveal the Desperate Hot Button
K — Keep on pushing buttons

1. Dangle Something for Nothing

What do conmen and conwomen do to seize your attention? They make you think you're getting a "steal."

I recently saw a documentary in which a conman on a street in England showed a toy that looked like it was dancing. This fake product was actually dancing because of a hidden, invisible thread. The conman was dangling something for nothing. The Entranced Buyer thought he was getting something worth $20 for only $5. That was the trick. The Entranced Buyer felt that he was getting $15 extra of value for his $5. What the Buyer really got was something worth nothing. Similarly, I know someone who purchased a copy of a Disney movie from a street vendor in San Francisco. She brought the copy home and it was unwatchable—and the street vendor was never seen again.

An old phrase goes, "A conman cannot con someone who is not looking for something for nothing."

How to Protect Yourself from "Dangle Something for Nothing"

Stop! Get on your cell phone and talk through the "deal" with someone you know who thinks clearly. Go home. Think about it. Do some research on the Internet. Listen to your gut feelings. If the salesman or conman is too insistent, get away from that Manipulator. Get quiet. Have a cup of water. Cool down. Break the Trance!

Break the Trance and Identify the Crucial Detail

Earlier, I mentioned that a Manipulator puts you into a trance. An added problem is that we put ourselves into a trance. For example, as you read this, are you thinking about your right toe? Most likely not (unless you stubbed your toe recently). The point is that we only focus on a tiny percentage of what is going on in our life.

Around fifteen years ago, I caused myself trouble because

I put myself into a trance. I discovered that under certain conditions, friendship can make you nearly deaf. Here's how: I was producing a song for a motion picture. A good friend was singing backup in the chorus. Because of our friendship, I wanted him to sound great. I completely missed the Crucial Detail. In this kind of situation, the Crucial Detail is that what truly counts is how the lead singer sounds! I made a song that I could not release. What a waste of time and money! I had put myself into a trance.

In any situation in which the Manipulator is "dangling something for nothing," we often fall into a trance and miss the Crucial Detail. The most important detail is *not* that we're saving money if we order before midnight tonight. What counts is whether the product creates a lasting, crucial benefit in our lives. And is the benefit of the product worth the cost? Some people even program themselves to make mistakes by saying, "I can't pass up a bargain." The bargain is *not* the Crucial Detail.

Secrets to Break the Trance

This is the process of B.R.E.A.K.S. It will help you remember the proven methods to break a trance.

B — Breathe
R — Relax
E — Envision
A — Act on aromas
K — Keep moving
S — Smile

Secret #1: Breathe

Remember Secret #1: Manipulators make you hurt and then offer the salve. The Manipulator wants to put you into a state of being that fills you with a sense of urgency and anxiety. Oh, no! I'm going to miss the sale!

Stop this highly vulnerable state. Take a deep breath. Do it now. Take a deep breath and let your belly "get fat" by filling it with air. As you breathe out, let your belly deflate. Breathe in through your nose and breathe out through your mouth. This is called belly-breathing. Repeat the actions of belly-breathing three times. Good. Now, do you feel different? Remember, when you are relaxed, you are strong.

End of Excerpt from
DARKEST SECRETS OF PERSUASION AND SEDUCTION MASTERS: HOW TO PROTECT YOURSELF AND TURN THE POWER TO GOOD
Copyright Tom Marcoux Media, LLC

Purchase your copy of this book (paperback or ebook) at Amazon.com or BarnesandNoble.com
See **Free Chapters** of Tom Marcoux's 23 books at http://amzn.to/ZiCTRj

ABOUT THE AUTHOR

Tom Marcoux helps people like you fulfill big dreams. Known as America's Communication Coach and TFG Thought Leader, Tom has authored 23 books with sales in 15 countries. One of his *Darkest Secrets* books rose to #1 on Amazon.com Hot New Releases in Business Life (and in Business Communication). He guides clients and audiences (IBM, Sun Microsystems, etc.) to success in job interviewing, public speaking, media relations, and branding. A member of the National Speakers Association, he is a professional coach and guest expert on TV, radio, and print, and was dubbed "the Personal Branding Instructor" by the *San Francisco Examiner*. Tom addressed National Association of Broadcasters' Conference six years running. With a degree in psychology, Tom is a guest lecturer at **Stanford University**, DeAnza, & California State University, and teaches public speaking, science fiction cinema/literature and comparative religion at Academy of Art University. Winner of a special award at the **Emmys**, Tom wrote, directed, and produced a feature film that the distributor took to the **Cannes film market**, and the film gained international distribution. He is engaged in book/film projects *Crystal Pegasus* (children's) and *TimePulse* (science fiction). See TomSuperCoach.com and Tom's well-received blog
   at www.BeHeardandBeTrusted.com

Tom Marcoux can help you with **speech writing** and **coaching for your best performance.**
As Tom says, *Make Your Speech a Pleasant Beach.*
Join Tom's Linkedin.com group: *Executive Public Speaking and Communication Power.*
Get a **Free** report: "9 Deadly Mistakes to Avoid for Your

Next Speech and 9 Surefire Methods" at
http://tomsupercoach.com/freereport9Mistakes4Speech.html

Tom Marcoux has trained CEOs, small business owners, and graduate students to speak with impact and gain audiences' tremendous approval and cooperation. *Learn how to present and get thunderous applause!*

"Tom, Thanks for your coaching and work with me on revising my speech at a major university. Working with you has been so enlightening for me. Through your gentle prodding and guidance I was able to write a speech that connects with the audience. I wish everyone could experience the transformation I have undergone. You have helped me discover the warm and compelling stories that now make my speech reach hearts and uplift minds. This was truly an empowering experience. I cannot thank you enough for your great assistance." — J.S.

"Tom Marcoux has been an NAB Conference favorite [speaker] for six years. And he is very energetic."
– John Marino,
Vice President, National Association of Broadcasters, Washington, D.C.

Become a fan of Tom's graphic novels/feature films:
Science fiction: *TimePulse*
www.facebook.com/timepulsegraphicnovel

Fantasy Thriller: *Jack AngelSword*
type "JackAngelSword" at Facebook.com

Children's Fantasy: *Crystal Pegasus*
www.facebook.com/crystalpegasusandrose
See **Free Chapters** of Tom Marcoux's 23 books at http://amzn.to/ZiCTRj

Special Offer Just for Readers of this Book:
Contact Tom Marcoux at tomsupercoach@gmail.com for special discounts on books, coaching, workshops and presentations. Just mention your experience with this book.

www.ingramcontent.com/pod-product-compliance
Lightning Source LLC
Chambersburg PA
CBHW060517100426
42743CB00009B/1349